D0327294

THE
AOC WAY

THE SECRETS OF ALEXANDRIA OCASIO-CORTEZ'S SUCCESS

CAROLINE FREDRICKSON

Skyhorse Publishing

Skyhorse Publishing books may be purchased in bulk at special discounts for sales promotion, corporate gifts, fund-raising, or educational purposes. Special editions can also be created to specifications. For details, contact the Special Sales Department, Skyhorse Publishing, 307 West 36th Street, 11th Floor, New York, NY 10018 or info@skyhorsepublishing.com.

Skyhorse® and Skyhorse Publishing® are registered trademarks of Skyhorse Publishing, Inc.®, a Delaware corporation.

Visit our website at www.skyhorsepublishing.com.

10 9 8 7 6 5 4 3 2 1

Library of Congress Cataloging-in-Publication Data is available on file.

Cover design by Brian Peterson
Cover photo credit Getty Images

ISBN: 978-1-5107-5208-5
Ebook ISBN 978-1-5107-5209-2

Printed in the United States of America

Contents

Introduction

In May 2019, I was at a conference in Flathead, Montana, focused on democracy and transparency in government, where activists and academics were discussing campaign finance reform and voting rights. During a panel discussion I was moderating on the challenges to making democracy more secure in America, a speaker lamented about how hard it can be to explain the impact of these issues to people outside the Beltway and connect dark money and the nefarious influence of special interests to the life experiences of average Americans. Not true, one of the panelists replied. He pointed out that newly elected congresswoman Alexandria Ocasio-Cortez had just done that very thing in a hearing on a pro-democracy bill. He had actually teed up a video of her questioning a witness that silenced the room—both in Congress when it happened and in Montana where we watched it. Ocasio-Cortez, popularly known as AOC, asked her questions in a way that illustrated the truly sordid nature of lobbying and dark money in Washington. With one question logically following another and building on the witness's answer, she showed how the dollars that flow from these special interests drive lawmakers to draft legislation (or even more commonly to use drafts written by the lobbyists themselves) that benefit those very interests—with the unsurprising result that the legislative process is actually undercutting our democracy and economic justice.

As part of his presentation on new communications strategies to advance democracy, the speaker on the panel used this clip of Ocasio-Cortez at the hearing to show how we could do our work better. AOC took her witness step by step through the process by which a lobbyist gives money to politicians and at the same time writes bills that the members of Congress introduce and vote for. It was so well done, was so easy to understand, and was so disturbing that the NowThis video of her questioning went viral. A subject that seemed esoteric and unrelatable was all of a sudden clear. And it wasn't just in explaining how the process worked that was so effective but also how AOC then connected this environment of slimy backroom backslapping and influence peddling to concrete outcomes that harm low-wage workers and vulnerable families in favor of banks and insurance companies. And the video was seen by millions of viewers across the country.[1] That was real impact.

At the end of the video, everyone in that room in Montana had a smile on their face. They looked at each other in happy amazement as if to say, "finally, someone who can bring these issues alive for new audiences and make them care deeply." To make real for the American people the true costs of having a political system where money buys not just access but outcomes has been a challenge for reformers. Here in one hearing, AOC had done it—and social media meant that people around the country could learn from her and share her clip with their friends and family. It had an exponential impact. One of AOC's real talents is an intuitive grasp of how to translate complex but important issues and to make them understandable; and, more importantly, to make them seem relevant to those who aren't glued to MSNBC day in, day out—to those who might have gotten turned off by politics because they didn't think their voice counted or because the system seemed too broken for them to make a difference.

Those of us in the fight for social justice struggle constantly with how to explain complex issues to a broad audience—and then to get people to care and to give them meaningful ways to take action. It may be the

---

1 Emily Stewart, "Alexandria Ocasio-Cortez's 'lightning round' on money in politics goes viral," *Vox*, February 8, 2019, https://www.vox.com/policy-and-politics/2019/2/8/18216884/alexandria-ocasio-cortez-video-campaign-finance.

single biggest challenge we face as advocates. Even when the public is generally on our side, we have difficulties in making our proposals to fix our broken democracy or address systemic breakdowns resonate with the public as forcefully as health care or economic distress. And then even if we can do that, we have the extra heavy lift of giving people something they can do about it—and then getting them to do it. In one short congressional hearing, Ocasio-Cortez was able to achieve much of this: expose a simple and compelling explanation of a problem, connect it to people's daily lives as a matter of urgency, propose real solutions, get people to pay attention. That the House moved forward on the legislation may have had something to do with the fact that House members heard from their constituents that the issue was of central importance. AOC gave a textbook lesson in advocacy. I, for one, was taking notes.

Like many people, I heard first about AOC after she beat an incumbent congressman in a Democratic primary. Initially, I found her intriguing as a harbinger (I hoped) of a more progressive and diverse leadership for the left. But as I spent more time following her career, I saw that she was more than that. She was transformative, a young and engaging social media influencer who could inject a spark into policy debates and be a force multiplier for democratic change.

As an advocate working on democracy and rule-of-law issues in Washington, DC, I had been focused for the duration of the Donald Trump presidency on trying to shore up our constitutional framework and fight back against corruption and self-dealing. Part of my work has involved writing and speaking out about the Russian interference in our elections in 2016 and hence on the investigation led by Special Counsel Robert Mueller at the Department of Justice. When President Trump's former attorney—or "fixer"—Michael Cohen was called to testify in front of a congressional committee, I was watching to see what he might say. I had few hopes for a real breakthrough since most congressional hearings just serve as vehicles for members of Congress to promote themselves rather than as real opportunities for advancing ideas or challenging policies. And to some extent that description was true for the Cohen hearing. But among the several new members who approached the hearing differently was Alexandria Ocasio-Cortez. She came well-prepared to use her question time to *ask questions! and to ask follow-up questions!* That may not seem unusual, but, trust me, it is. A typical member uses the time for pontificating or bloviating, rarely getting to a question and instead making a statement. Even when they do ask a question, they almost never pay attention to the answer. Not only did she ask questions and build on what she learned through further inquiries, but she used her time the way a good lawyer in a trial would—to lead a witness through the evidence in order to establish the proof behind her arguments, and, in this case, to outline areas for further investigation. It was a masterful showing. Charlotte Alter, in a profile she wrote for *Time*, exclaimed "She's a political phenomenon: part activist, part legislator, arguably the best storyteller in the party since Barack Obama and perhaps the only Democrat right now with the star power to challenge President Donald Trump's."[2] After AOC was done asking her questions—along with several other new members—the Democrats had a road map to pursue investigations into Trump's alleged efforts to hide or diminish the value of his assets to fend off creditors and inflate them to get more loans and insurance payments. The sequencing of her questions was crisp, specific, and actionable.

Frankly, I was mesmerized. In a spurt of writing, I drafted an opinion piece for the *New York Times*. Most of the paper's coverage focused on Cohen and his statement implicating President Trump in crimes and unethical behavior, but my main interest was on sending a message to other politicians—"Learn from her!" If more Democrats did what AOC did in a hearing, congressional committees could actually make those events into productive moments for engaging and educating the public and also establishing a real basis for further hearings and investigations based on testimony and other evidence uncovered in a hearing. The *Times* published my piece, entitled "How Alexandria Ocasio-Cortez Won the Cohen Hearing." (The title was not quite accurate, as I mentioned a few others who similarly avoided

2   Charlotte Alter, "'Change Is Closer Than We Think.' Inside Alexandria Ocasio-Cortez's Unlikely Rise," *Time*, March 21, 2019, http://time.com/longform/alexandria-ocasio-cortez-profile/.

grandstanding in favor of evidence-gathering.) The piece, originally only in the online publication, quickly got over one million views and ended up in the hard copy of the paper the next day. At the end of the week it was still one of the top two most-read *New York Times* articles in that period. I would like to think that was because of my rhetoric and the beauty of my prose, but in reality it was the star power of AOC that caused the piece to go viral. Yet people read the piece not only because AOC is a hot property right now, but also because it challenged the common assumption that she is a flash in the pan, of little substance, all social media and no real-life engagement. Anyone watching the hearing would know that none of that is true. And this hearing was not an aberration but in fact the way the young congresswoman operates in Washington. She's careful and thorough, does her home-work, and works to have an impact. But she combines that discipline and interest in making a difference with an uncanny ability to break down issues to their simplest parts and explain complex subjects in language that makes them accessible and interesting to the public—and does the more important part of even getting people to take action. This has been true of her hearing appearances on legislation to protect our democracy as well as her use of Twitter and Instagram to demonstrate the impact of cli-mate change on our daily lives. She's a communicator, a translator, and a motivator. And she's exciting to watch.

Her commitment to the issues transcends partisan identifications. When she discovered that Senator Ted Cruz from Texas, one of the most conservative members of the Senate, shared her view that members of Congress should face a permanent ban on lobbying, she reached out to him to join her in sponsoring legislation. And he did. And then she looked for other Republicans who similarly view the revolving door as unbridled corruption. She found Chip Roy in the House and Senator Brian Schatz, a Democrat from Hawaii who signed on as Cruz's Senate cosponsor. AOC tweeted her excitement about the bipartisan effort and retweeted Roy's commitment to join her on the bill: "Okay, with @brianschatz+ @tedcruz we've got at least one D-R team in the Senate to ban members becoming lobbyists, & myself w/ @chiproytx makes at least one D-R team in the House. And that's just in a few hours - there will surely be more from both parties to sign on. Nice."[3] What is clear is that AOC is authentic and lives her values. She is a committed liberal, feminist, and believer in economic justice, but when she finds a conservative who agrees with her on an issue, she will work with that person because what matters is making a difference. Some might find such a quality heroic. In fact, Alexandria Ocasio-Cortez is now even a comic book hero. Soon after she started in Congress, Devil's Due, a comic book publisher, announced its latest product:

---

3   Alexandria Ocasio-Cortez, *Twitter*, May 30, 2019, https://twitter .com/AOC/status/1134227048686338048.

Alexandria Ocasio-Cortez and the Freshman Force: New Party Who Dis? It's Alexandria Ocasio-Cortez and the "Freshman Force" of Congress vs. the establishment in this all new commemorative comic! . . . From the house that brought you Barack the Barbarian: No F#¢*s Left! Featuring comics from various artists and bonus activities and games. Grab a hamberder and cup of covfefe and prepare to enjoy this read![4]

Dressed in a glamorous white suit, astride a dead, red elephant, AOC holds out her cell phone like a magic weapon of justice. Apart from the ugly imagery of an elephant killing, which brings up bad memories of Donald Trump's sons' horrendous hunting expeditions in Africa, it is an inspiring cover.

AOC is indeed a superhero, but she's also reliably human and approachable. She's truly got the Superman/Clark Kent schtick down (including the glasses)—it comes out in her ability to talk directly to people about issues in their daily lives while at the same time participate in congressional hearings and briefings at a level equal to or superior to those who have served decades on the Hill. Her impact has already been outsized—she has successfully pushed many of the Democratic candidates for president to take a stronger stance on climate change, including embracing the Green New Deal. She worked

---

4 "Alexandria Ocasio-Cortez and the Freshman Force: New Party Who Dis?" *Devil's Due Comics*, accessed August 6, 2019, http://www.ocasiocomic.com/#/.

with local activists in New York to prevent Amazon from opening a major office there that was feared would raise housing and transportation costs for average people. And she's brought public attention to esoteric issues like campaign finance reform where she was able to build a large audience for her clear and dramatic explanation of how lobbying and corporate money influence legislative outcomes. Even her lipstick brand has gone viral, once she mentioned it on Twitter.[5]

But there's a downside to all of this fame and attention. Apart from the fact that she's now recognized everywhere she goes—"I miss being able to go outside in sweats," she told a *Time* reporter, "I can't go anywhere in public and just be a person without a lot of people watching everything I do." Certainly, it is a challenge to process the change from being a bartender struggling to earn a living wage to the hero of a comic book, the star of a documentary, and a political rising star. That's head-spinning. But there are worse downsides. While she's got a large following on social media and many who admire her, she's also the subject of visceral hatred from some on the right who see her as epitomizing the change they fear: she's a woman of color, urban, hip, young, and progressive. And she's not just progressive. She calls herself a democratic socialist, as do many in her age group. Her profile captures the evolution of the United States

---

5   Charlotte Alter, "'Change Is Closer Than We Think.' Inside Alexandria Ocasio-Cortez's Unlikely Rise," *Time,* March 21, 2019, http://time.com/longform/alexandria-ocasio-cortez-profile/.

and its political landscape—from white male–dominated to a nation where women and people of color have a role to play and are a growing force. She's challenging both white supremacy and our new gilded age's version of capitalism. And striking a nerve. She's trolled on Twitter and endlessly defamed on right-wing media, seemingly the only Democratic politician in Washington on certain days, so obsessed are some in their criticisms of her. Some on the right hate her so much she has received death threats.[6]

And it's not just the far right that fears and hates her. Some Democrats think she's moving too far and too fast. They think her policy proposals are too radical and prefer an incrementalist approach. But she's impatient. "By the time legislation actually gets through, it is five years from now," she told reporter Charlotte Alter. "So everything we introduce needs to have 2025 or our kids in mind." Unlike most politicians who focus on the next election and thus only on the bills that they can introduce or pass in two-year blocks of time, she has a longer-term horizon. She's looking for real change. She doesn't see this approach so much as an internal Democratic Party schism but as an indicator of where the country is going. "There's always this talk about division within the Democratic Party, ideological differences," she said. "But I actually think they're generational differences. Because the America we grew up in is nothing like the America our parents or our grandparents grew up

---

6 Ibid.

in."[7] Her generation and those after hers haven't had the same belief in the American dream and endless opportunity. They see their future not as one of growing prosperity but one where they will face financial stresses and struggle to have a middle-class life. At the same time, these younger people fear the coming impact of climate change on their lives and well-being.

Stepping up to do her part fighting the climate crisis, AOC partnered with the Sunrise Movement, an "army of young people to stop climate change." Together they released "A Message from the Future with Alexandria Ocasio-Cortez." In an email to activists, the group announced that the "video . . . is about how we got where we are today and what could be possible over the coming decade if we come together and fight for a Green New Deal."[8] The message: we don't have time to wait. For AOC, that imperative translates into an agenda of big dreams and high hopes. How can we create an America where the powerless and the vulnerable have a voice, where economic prosperity is shared more fairly, where our rivers and lakes are clean and our air is breathable now and in the future? If the elders in power won't address the problem, then it must be the role of younger people to force a response.

It's a big task but one that has to be taken on—or else. And one that she is optimistic about. "I used to be

---

7 Ibid.
8 "A Message from the Future with Alexandria Ocasio-Cortez," Sunrise Movement blast email, April 17, 2019 (on file with author).

much more cynical about how much was up against us," she told *Time*. "I think I've changed my mind. Because I think that change is a lot closer than we think."[9] She argues that the rising electorate of young and diverse voters will in fact make this change happen—it has the growing numbers and political engagement to make a real impact.

And she's got the data to show it. In response to those who say Democrats should pay more attention to disaffected white working-class men, she says that's not the answer. According to Ocasio-Cortez, "This is why I say that expanding the electorate is a more effective strategy than burning to win over a tiny slice of people. It's entitled to demand 'vote blue no matter who' - no matter how 'right' that is." Her tweet continued, "You HAVE to deliver a real platform that improves people's lives." She attached a bar graph to her tweet showing the bigger problem in the 2016 presidential election was not the Trump-Obama voters (a "unicorn" if there ever was one!) but the Obama-nobody voters—the progressives who stayed home in 2016 altogether. She then quoted a tweet by Alex Kotch, saying "This is pretty astounding, and could happen again if another Democratic centrist becomes the presidential nominee."

AOC concluded, "& I mean improve ALL people's lives, not only 'swing voters' lives. If all you want to talk

---

9 Charlotte Alter, "'Change Is Closer Than We Think.' Inside Alexandria Ocasio-Cortez's Unlikely Rise," *Time*, March 21, 2019, http://time.com/longform/alexandria-ocasio-cortez-profile/.

about is wages but not the wage gap; marijuana but not criminal justice reform; trade deals but not labor; feminism but not trans rights, it's YOU diminishing your electorate, not them."[10]

If the Democratic Party leadership actually does pay attention to the data and connect the dots, then they will start to look at the issues that face the real Democratic base—and the emerging majority of Americans. So despite the hatred from the right and the effort to tamp her down by Democratic moderates, she still has—and inspires—hope for a better future, one with fewer guns and better schools, with fairer wages and more economic equity, with greater tolerance and a healthy environment. We can hope, can't we?

Alexandria Ocasio-Cortez's life has certainly become more complicated since she left the Bronx. But it doesn't seem like AOC has any regrets, apart from an understandable sadness about the loss of her private life. She has high hopes and big dreams, and there's no doubt at least some of them are going to be realized. And she also has identified major threats and issued a call for Americans to take action and take it now to avert catastrophe. I hope she can be successful there, too.

This book takes life lessons from this rising star,

---

10   Alexandria Ocasio-Cortez, Twitter, May 31, 2019, https://twitter.com/aoc/status/1134459280579604480?s=11.

Alexandria Ocasio-Cortez—already known to millions of people by her acronym "AOC"—that readers can apply to their own lives. In an incredibly short time, the young member of Congress has galvanized the country on issues of national importance. Forcing Democrats to confront climate change and income inequality, she is upending conventional wisdom about how young women, especially women of color, are supposed to behave. Her background, including a family that fell out of the middle class due to health-care challenges, has driven her to champion those on the margins, such as low-wage workers, immigrants, people of color, and younger people who face a future of climate disruption and instability. While she's become a comic book hero, an influencer on social media, and a leading light in Congress, AOC's examples are instructive for those of us, especially women, who aren't in the limelight or known to the public as is the now-famous congresswoman.

Meant not exactly as a biography and not exactly as self-help, this book aims to marry the two by drawing lessons from AOC and attempting to distill the "AOC way." Some of the readers may have read other books directed to women that aim to give them skills to navigate the workforce and life more generally, telling them to look to themselves to solve problems. I found that frustrating and obtuse—only public policy can provide systemic changes, and many women are not in any position to "lean in." In my book *Under the Bus*, I state it bluntly:

[W]hile the media debate "opt out" and "lean in," the real focus should be those who are "left out." Women work, and increasingly they are filling jobs with few benefits, low wages, and unpredictable schedules. Even middle-class Americans are suffering from the consequences of the changes in our workplaces and the need for two incomes. Our workplace laws threw women of color under the bus from the beginning, but we will all get run over if we don't reinvent our system to get everyone on board.[11]

What Ocasio-Cortez does brilliantly is to understand that women must stand together both in fighting for policy solutions and for each other as friends, colleagues, coworkers, and community members. She recognizes that any hope for justice and equality for women must include both systemic nationwide changes that need to occur to allow women to thrive, especially women of color and women who face economic and other challenges, but also the small but meaningful ways we can help each other directly. In other words, the human touch. Feminists in the 1970s were credited with coming up with the expression, "the personal is political"—that's what it means. If we live our lives according to our values—treating other women with dignity, praising their successes, supporting them in

---

11   Caroline Fredrickson, *Under the Bus* (New York: The New Press, 2015).

their battles, comforting them when they are down, and fighting alongside them to change the world—our politics will also change. So it is not either/or but both/and. Personal commitment, political action.

In five chapters, this book weaves substantive issues and AOC's experiences to understand how she so quickly came to dominate media coverage in America but also to drive real change in what seems like a lightning flash. AOC has demonstrated some key values and commitments on her way to success, such as believing in yourself and not letting haters take you off course; working hard and being prepared to prove your talents; bringing your experiences to your work by not forgetting how you got where you are; challenging the status quo; and staying true to your friends and allies. She's upended assumptions about what groups like youth, specifically young people of color; people from economically distressed backgrounds; immigrant families; and others are capable of—or how they should behave. She's not been willing to sit back and listen to the direction of her elders. Time is of the essence, she knows, for our nation and the world to deal with climate change, economic inequality, and corporate greed.

At a time when so many of us are anxious about what is happening in our country and frankly terrified that worse might be coming in the future, Alexandria Ocasio-Cortez and her story can give us some hope and keep us from despair. She's not giving up; nor should we. And, beyond the political and policy proposals, AOC also has a lot to say to women and others who have not had control of the levers of power in this country. Her example can help us become bolder and stronger but also allows us to stand together so that even the shy can be mighty. These are lessons in how to exert our power over politicians, how to stay true to our values and our friends, and how to believe in ourselves. She says to each of us, "we are all wonder women."

Wonder women will reshape America. AOC recognizes that we cannot fight alone and win. Each of us is necessary for the collective good. That is why she stands up for her sisters—and her brothers—when they need someone to take their side. And that's why she also uses her platform to celebrate the successes and accomplishments of women and progressive leaders. She shouts it from the rooftops—or the twenty-first-century version: she tweets and Instagrams about it. She works collaboratively with her fellow freshmen in the House and with senators who have been in office since before she was born.

Since being elected, Ocasio-Cortez has faced death threats and insults. Her staff have to control access to her office and keep her schedule under wraps. But she persists. Because to give up and surrender to the bullies would mean that they had won. And to give up and surrender would suggest to other young women, to people of color, to the vulnerable and impoverished, to the disabled and the dismissed, that they are really not of equal status. And to give up and surrender would allow this vision of "we the people" to be abandoned.

But that's not the AOC Way. The AOC Way is for all of us to have a voice and a value, whatever our age, color, gender identity, religion, or other attribute.

CHAPTER ONE
Dance Your Own Dance

"It takes courage to grow up and turn out to be who you really are."

—E. E. Cummings

ONE REASON AOC HAS A special place in our hearts is her joyful approach to her work, which is coupled with—and seems to sustain—her fierce belief in fighting for justice. This independent spirit is what has captured the interest, the admiration, and even the fascination of her fan base. She's really and truly herself, defiantly herself, not scripted by or bullied by others to fit some mold they deem appropriate for a young woman. It's not mere self-confidence, which is admirable in itself, but the fact that she seems comfortable in her skin. For women, who are constantly rated and judged for their looks, clothes, social skills, smarts, and a million other things, that's a difficult achievement, especially for someone who is young, a minority, and is shaking up an arena long dominated by white men—politics.

AOC has marched forthrightly into the halls of Congress. Rather than allowing criticism by mainstream politicians or right-wing trolls to throw her off balance, she decided to run for office, and not dogcatcher but United States Congresswoman. Challenging an incumbent, she had everyone against her. The mainstream party rallied behind her opponent, and the monied interests filled his coffers, while Ocasio-Cortez scraped by on volunteer help and elbow grease. But she was determined, she persisted, and she won. Her presence online as well as in hearings illuminates her determination to make her own way and not to play by the traditional rules. In the hidebound world of Congress, newer members of the body wait their turn to speak out and even then only get a little airtime. But AOC came to the Hill with things to say and much to accomplish, and she's off and running. She has used her powerful social media presence not just to clap back at her critics but also to use her platform to educate the broader public on issues from climate change to campaign finance reform, tax policy to health care. She's also generously given her fellow House Democrats a primer on the use of social media.

She's serious on the details of policy but lighthearted and even joyful in how she presents the issues. She recognizes that a committee hearing doesn't have to be dull and pointless. But those who spend time in DC know that, in fact, hearings often become a showcase for the show pony, in other words, an opportunity for politicians just to give another speech about themselves rather than use a hearing to achieve a policy goal. AOC sees their potential to make a case for a point of view, and that means asking witnesses serious questions, with an eye to laying out an argument. Not only does that better explain policy proposals, identify who's on which side, and get evidence into the record, it's much better theater. And we all know that the only theater that is successful is one where the audience stays to see the end of the play.

Big scoop from right-wing conspiracy theorist AnonymousQ: Alexandria Ocasio-Cortez made a selfie video in college showing her dancing. With classmates from Boston University, AOC performed an homage to the iconic *The Breakfast Club* scene set to Phoenix's "Lisztomania." AnonymousQ thought he had snagged the ultimate gotcha video, and introduced it with the snarky note: "Here is America's favorite commie know-it-all acting like the clueless nitwit she is......High School video of 'Sandy' Ocasio-Cortez pic.twitter.com/s723Vga9zF." His tone dripped venom, patronizing and dismissive all at once. Oops. Not a good idea to tangle with AOC and her friends.

AOC's Twitter followers had a field day. The posts were funny and biting:

Zach Schonfeld: "Working on my big new scoop: an interview with Alexandria Ocasio-Cortez's 9th grade math teacher, who reveals she once confused Cosine and Tangent in 2004."

Matt Oswalt: "In an alley on K Street a young Republican hands a briefcase to a shadowy figure. He opens it to find it filled with cash. He hands the Republican a preschool drawing by Alexandria Ocasio-Cortez where she drew ... outside the lines. The Republican smiles and walks off into the night."[12]

Still others took the video and set it to new music. In a newly launched Twitter account, @aoc_dances, an amused twitterverse took the footage and gleefully had AOC dance to dozens of different songs.[13] And then Ocasio-Cortez herself got in on the act. AOC did not get embarrassed nor apologize. Apparently, she thinks liberals can have fun and be fun. So instead of hiding or denying or explaining that she had been younger when she made the video, she embraced it. You might even say she flaunted it. Creating a new video of herself dancing, AOC in essence smiled back at her critics, blew them a kiss, and said "I dance, that's who I am. Deal with it." Posting her new dance video on January 4, 2019, AOC danced to "War (What Is It Good

12   Caitlin MacNeal, "Right-Wing Twitter Account Reveals AOC Once . . . Danced In College," *Talking Points Memo*, January 3, 2019, https://talkingpointsmemo.com/news/ocasio-cortez-video-dancing-backlash.
13   Sophie Lewis, "Ocasio-Cortez's College Dance Video Has Now Been Set to All Your Favorite Songs," *CBS News*, January 4, 2019, https://www.cbsnews.com/news/aoc-dances-twitter-account-alexandria-ocasio-cortez-dance-video/.

For?)" by Edwin Starr. AOC tweeted, "I hear the GOP thinks women dancing are scandalous," she wrote in the caption. "Wait till they find out Congresswomen dance too! Have a great weekend everyone :)" Immediately, her video went viral, and in less than an hour had more than 100,000 retweets.[14]

A PR News account admired how AOC used a jujitsu move to "turn a smear attempt into a statement on women's freedoms," deeming it "a perfect case study in making the most out of a potential crisis."[15] And Jenny Hollander commented in *Marie Claire*, "We're less than one week into 2019, and you probably need a break already." She went through the laundry list of big events, from Elizabeth Warren's annnouncement of her candidacy for president, to the partial government shutdown, and the never-ending and concerning tweets from the president. And then, she said, there was that "scandal over an unearthed video of brand-new congresswoman Alexandria Ocasio-Cortez dancing with her friends in high school. To me, this video says that she's cool *and* smart *and* fun, but some conservatives were intimidated because they'll never be able to match her dance prowess. Or something."[16] One reporter on *Talking Points Memo* asked, "Ocasio-Cortez dances and

14   Ibid.

15   Sophie Maerowitz, "3 Pillars of Alexandria Ocasio-Cortez's Digital Domination," *PR News*, January 7, 2019, https://www.prnewsonline.com/aoc-digital-domination.

16   Jenny Hollander, "Here's Alexandria Ocasio-Cortez Dancing to All of Your Favorite Songs," *Marie Claire*, January 4, 2019, https://www.marieclaire.com/politics/a25749419/alexandra-ocasio-cortez-dancing-twitter/.

the wingnut brigade is right out of Footloose. Aren't they the same folks who accuse liberals of not being fun?"[17]

Ultimately, AOC won the social media war by staying true to herself. AOC even found joy in the attacks, tweeting out a smiley face with tears from laughter, "Why do people think they can mess with Bronx women without getting roasted? They act as though our borough hasn't been perfecting the clapback game since the Sugarhill Gang y'all just found it on Twitter."[18] She is cool and smart and fun—but she also calls on us to join her. Her coolness is not a mean girl coolness, sharp and hard and designed to draw lines between the in-crowd and the rest of us. Her coolness is fun, joyful, and inclusive. Come dancing. . . .

Alexandria Ocasio-Cortez stays true to herself. She dances her own dance without embarrassment or denial. How did she become someone who could respond to public criticism with a joyous response? Why, when so many young women suffer from Internet abuse and trolls, was she able to withstand and shame her anonymous stalkers? And how did she gain the confidence to challenge a long-serving Democratic incumbent in the primary when she had no experience, the full-throated opposition of the

---

17   Caitlin MacNeal, "Right-Wing Twitter Account Reveals AOC Once . . . Danced In College," *Talking Points Memo*, January 3, 2019, https://talkingpointsmemo.com/news/ocasio-cortez-video-dancing-backlash.

18   Tweet from Ocasio-Cortez, January 20, 2019, https://twitter.com/aoc/status/1087025397211058183?lang=en.

mainstream party leaders and funders, including incoming Speaker Nancy Pelosi? Her resilience and insouciance are a lesson for all of us—but where does it come from?

Ocasio-Cortez began her campaign while waiting tables and tending bar at Flats Fix, a taqueria in New York City's Union Square. Unlike many candidates, she had not spent time in a career that made her lots of money or toiling in the backwaters of Democratic politics, working her way up the ladder. She had been struggling for tips to pay the rent in the kind of job done by many vulnerable women. "For 80 percent of this campaign, I operated out of a paper grocery bag hidden behind that bar," she told *Bon Appétit*.[19] Rather than "wait her turn" as she was supposed to do, AOC thought it was enough that Joe Crowley was not right for the district and not progressive enough for the times, as she herself was. She filed to run against him. And she won. She faced a financial disadvantage, saying, "You can't really beat big money with more money. You have to beat them with a totally different game."[20] Her campaign spent $194,000 to the Crowley campaign's $3.4 million. That's an eighteen-to-one differential in terms of financial resources and really illustrates the Alexandria versus Goliath battle she had to fight.

But AOC was right. Crowley was not right for the

---

19   Hilary Cadigan, "Alexandria Ocasio-Cortez Learned Her Most Important Lessons from Restaurants," *Bon Appetit,* November 7, 2019, https://www.bonappetit.com/story/alexandria-ocasio-cortez-lessons-from-restaurants.

20   "Alexandria Ocasio-Cortez," November 21, 2018, *AccessFeminism,* https://accessfeminism.com/2018/11/21/alexandria-ocasio-cortez/.

district. A long-serving politician, he was close to New York City political brokers, and some thought he might actually become the next Democratic House Speaker (certainly *he* thought so). And even though he had spoken out critically on some of Trump's policies and for some liberal policy proposals, he also had taken money from Wall Street's banking interests and did not really understand his own district. AOC, on the other hand, knew her neighbors, had lived a life closer to the hardscrabble circumstances faced by many of them, and had decided to take only small donations and reject PAC contributions.[21] In an interview with *The Intercept*, AOC said, "This [race] is actually about electing Democrats whose financial interests are aligned with their communities' interests."[22]

Crowley had gotten close to Wall Street during his time in the House, drifting away from the union support that had fueled his early career. He had spent many years shaking hands with the bankers and hedge fund managers who fill the coffers of both Republican and Democratic politicians. That closeness got him into trouble during the efforts to bail out the financial industry after the Great Recession. In the perfect embodiment of political quid pro quo, Crowley took money from Wall Street lobbyists

---

21 Elaine Godfrey, "Joe Crowley Just Played into Alexandria Ocasio-Cortez's Hands," *The Atlantic,* February 21, 2019, https://www.theatlantic.com/politics/archive/2019/02/joe-crowleys-lobbying-job-plays-aocs-hands/583174/.
22 Aida Chavez and Ryan Grim, "A Primary Against the Machine: A Bronx Activist Looks to Dethrone Joseph Crowley, the King of Queens," *The Intercept,* May 22, 2018 https://theintercept.com/2018/05/22/joseph-crowley-alexandria-ocasio-cortez-new-york-primary/.

and immediately voted to protect the banks from more onerous regulations. Crowley found himself caught up in an ethics probe, when the proximity of his vote against the regulations and acceptance of campaign contributions raised the interest of the Office of Congressional Ethics, which sent the case to the House Committee on Ethics to continue the probe. The Ethics Committee ultimately found no wrongdoing.[23] Even though Crowley escaped any liability for ethics violations, his actions didn't smell good—and illustrated how his path had diverged from the working people of his district.

Not recognizing that he was increasingly out of step with his constituents, Crowley bragged about knowing how to play the Washington money game. He was proud of his relationship with Wall Street, boasting to *The New York Daily News*, "Many people here in Washington view me as an important figure."[24] What he didn't seem to get was that for people in the Bronx and Queens, he was an increasingly irrelevant figure.

Named as the finance vice chair for the Democratic Congressional Campaign Committee by his ally Nancy Pelosi, Crowley played the familiar role of bringing in cash and distributing it to his fellow Democrats in the House. It's a good way to get support from other politicians and

23   Ibid.
24   Benjamin Lesser, "Queens Congressman Joe Crowley's Campaign Funds Under Investigation in Ethics Probe," *New York Daily News*, June 27, 2010, https://www.nydailynews.com/new-york/queens/queens-congressman-joe-crowley-campaign-funds-investigation-ethics-probe-article-1.182878.

to build up chits that can be used for other purposes. He was good at the money chase, eventually earning a promotion for his fund-raising prowess, becoming the chair of the House Democratic Caucus. In 2017 and 2018, he served as a contact for the conservative wing of the party, helping candidates in different parts of the country, as he hoped to displace Pelosi as speaker (that's where the chits come in). But then he faced a primary challenge, something he had not faced since 2004.

Many commentators attributed AOC's ultimate victory in the race to the changing demographics of the district. And, at least in part, that might be true. AOC better reflected a population that had grown increasingly brown and black since Crowley had been elected. Residents of the district, made up of parts of Queens and the Bronx, found a young woman of Puerto Rican heritage to be a relatable candidate. The district has a population that is 49 percent Hispanic and less than 20 percent white. But there was more at issue than race. In fact, AOC spoke to people in a language they found compelling and had a life experience they could identify with. She was not just the form but much more importantly she was the substance. She could understand the lives of her neighbors and could appreciate their struggles in a personal way (something we used to call "empathy" until Republicans attacked President Obama for suggesting that it was an important quality in his selection of judicial nominees. And proving the point that Democratic politicians too often run from their best instincts, they joined in the chorus . . . but I digress). And even more importantly, her policy responses appealed to them. As Ocasio-Cortez herself told the *New York Times* right after the election, she won because of her ideas, not because of her race. "It would be a huge mistake to just say that this election happened because X demographics live here. That is to absolutely miss the entire point of what we just accomplished," Ocasio-Cortez said.[25] Ideas actually matter—and especially when they are genuine, not poll-tested and packaged, but coming from thoughtful consideration of data and lived experience.

She ran on a platform of economic justice, similar to elements of the platform of Bernie Sanders's presidential campaign, where she had volunteered as an organizer. Her main proposals included Medicare for All, a jobs guarantee, abolishing the Immigration and Customs Enforcement Agency (ICE), and limiting campaign donations. "What I see is that the Democratic Party takes working class communities for granted, they take people of color for granted and they just assume that we're going to turn out no matter how bland or half-stepping these proposals are," Ocasio-Cortez said to the *New York Times* shortly before the primary.[26] Her ideas were nei-

25 Shane Goldmacher, "An Upset in the Making: Why Joe Crowley Never Saw Defeat Coming," *New York Times,* June 27, 2018, https://www.nytimes.com/2018/06/27/nyregion/ocasio-cortez-crowley-primary-upset.html.

26 Shane Goldmacher and Jonathan Martin, "Alexandria Ocasio-Cortez Defeats Joseph Crowley in Major Democratic House Upset, *New York Times,* June 26, 2018, https://www.nytimes.com/2018/06/26/nyregion/joseph-crowley-ocasio-cortez-democratic-primary.html.

ther milquetoast nor partial steps, but fully baked major reforms for key parts of our economy.

Indeed, AOC found support for her platform throughout the district, and even produced a higher vote margin in Crowley's home base of Queens than she did in winning the Bronx. Crowley was doubly humiliated, losing overall but especially losing his base voters. "She won virtually everywhere," said Steven Romalewski, a researcher at the Center for Urban Research at the City University of New York Graduate Center, to the *New York Times*. Romalewski pointed to her strong vote count in Astoria, with a white population of nearly 50 percent. "Her strongest support came from areas that were not predominantly Hispanic," Mr. Romalewski said.[27] AOC's victory should put the lie to the idea that women and people of color have a limited appeal beyond women and people of color—a refrain we hear all the time in the campaign for president in the upcoming 2020 election.

When he saw polls showing that he was not known by his constituents and not much liked if he was known, Crowley finally geared up his campaign in May of 2018. He inundated voters with brochures and mailings, which had the result of actually raising awareness of his opponent, Ocasio-Cortez. AOC, always sensitive to opportunities, decided to tell voters about herself through a video

---

27   Shane Goldmacher, "An Upset in the Making: Why Joe Crowley Never Saw Defeat Coming," *New York Times*, June 27, 2018, https://www.nytimes.com/2018/06/27/nyregion/ocasio-cortez-crowley-primary-upset.html.

she put out that same month, calling herself this "girl from the Bronx." She wanted to make it clear to her neighbors how different she was from the incumbent and how much more attention she would pay to their interests, as opposed to Wall Street's interests. In two minutes, she related how she took the subway while Crowley took a car. She was the straphanger and he was the town car rider—it was an important metaphor for the race. Crowley tried his own video, which showed how far he was out of step with his voters. "The one thing about my life experience," he said in the opening, "is the ability to put myself in other people's shoes." Apparently, it was not convincing. Only 90,000 people watched Crowley's video, while over half a million tuned into the AOC biographical video.[28] While he claimed to applaud the changing demographics of the district, AOC embodied them.

Eventually Crowley recognized that he was lagging behind due to more than just the changing demographics. Growing more alarmed, the congressman also began to see that his district was much more progressive than he was and was aligned with AOC's political views. Finger to the wind, he began to adjust. Just as he had been able to move away from labor and embrace the financial sector, Crowley now moved left. All of a sudden, Crowley supported Medicare for All. AOC didn't buy it—and made sure the voters knew who was the real health-care advocate. "When I launched my campaign on an unapologetic advocacy for 'Medicare for All,' within two weeks, he co-sponsored the legislation," Ocasio-Cortez said to *The Intercept*. "That's when people first started noticing how sensitive he was to our race, how sensitive he was to this challenge." Crowley tried to claim his shift in position had nothing to do with his opponent, and a campaign staffer said, "She's not making him any more progressive; he's always been a progressive advocate."[29] Evidence to the contrary: his positions showed rapid evolution after AOC got in the race and began to move past him in the polls.

After Ocasio-Cortez called for getting rid of ICE, suddenly Crowley too began to attack the department. On criminal justice reform, a bigger and bigger issue in Democratic politics, AOC called out Crowley for getting funding from former New York City Mayor Michael Bloomberg, saying "so we got the guy who created stop and frisk, who's paying the representative of Rikers Island to continue this racket of incarcerating black and brown people in New York City." Bloomberg had held an event at his glitzy abode in Manhattan, asking invitees to pony up amounts from $1,000 to $2,700 all the way to $5,400. Indignant that Crowley seemed to have forgotten that the district included Rikers Island jail, AOC reminded the voters that the monied interests supporting Crowley had not just failed to support criminal justice reform but actively opposed it. She made the point to

---

29 Aida Chavez and Ryan Grim, "A Primary Against the Machine: A Bronx Activist Looks to Dethrone Joseph Crowley, the King of Queens," *The Intercept*, May 22, 2018 https://theintercept.com/2018/05/22/joseph-crowley-alexandra-ocasio-cortez-new-york-primary/.

The Intercept that she wasn't running so the district could elect "just any old Democrat." Crowley, like other Wall Street Democrats, no longer stood up for his constituents, and those elected officials often "take the very same money as Republicans." Crowley's second biggest source of funding was the Blackstone Group, a major Trump supporter.

"This is actually about electing Democrats whose financial interests are aligned with their communities' interests," Ocasio-Cortez said. Crowley, she said, had forgotten his district, representing special interests "at odds with everything that this community needs." His changes in position on Medicare for All or ICE, she argued, could not be relied on, because his financial ties were stronger than any momentary and opportunistic policy switch—it was only "face value, [nothing] deeper than a re-election bid."[30] And that was why the voters liked Ocasio-Cortez; her appeal was that her views were deeply held. Even if voters didn't agree with her, they knew that she wasn't just putting out policy ideas after her consultants did polling and message testing to craft an appealing platform. AOC made it hard for Crowley to escape his history of cozying up to big donors and banking interests by showing voters what she believed in.

AOC won that campaign the way she has lived her

---

30 Aida Chavez and Ryan Grim, "A Primary Against the Machine: A Bronx Activist Looks to Dethrone Joseph Crowley, the King of Queens," *The Intercept*, May 22, 2018 https://theintercept.com/2018/05/22/joseph-crowley-alexandria-ocasio-cortez-new-york-primary/.

life, with authenticity and true passion. Her voters wanted someone who was "real," who understood their lives and struggles, and who would be there for them—not just during campaign season but all the time. They wanted someone to represent them, defend their interests, and expand their opportunities. AOC has only served part of one term in the House of Representatives, but she continues to be relatable and approachable, something that comes as close to a brand as anything.

But Alexandria Ocasio-Cortez did not limit her effervescence to the campaign nor to college videos. She continued to live fully, using her positive energy to help others as she began her role as a congresswoman. Sophie Weiner, writing for *Splinter News*, exulted, "It's logical to fear that any politician with a semblance of humanity will eventually disappoint us. But somehow, in defiance of our low expectations, freshman Congresswoman Alexandria Ocasio-Cortez just keeps getting cooler. This evening she became perhaps the first Congressperson to ever appear on a Twitch stream, and *certainly* the first Congressperson to guest on a charity Twitch stream supporting trans rights."[31] AOC, being herself as usual,

---

31 Sophie Weiner, "AOC Breaks the Internet by Dropping in on Charity Twitch Stream for Trans Kids," *Splinter News*, January 20, 2019, https://splinternews.com/aoc-breaks-the-internet-by-dropping-in-on-charity-twitc-1831913167.

decided to join Youtuber H.bomberguy to talk about trans children and help raise money for Mermaid, a nonprofit dedicated to their rights. H.bomberguy had embarked on an "epic, 50-hours-and-counting *Donkey Kong 64* stream," to help generate funds, and AOC was just the help he needed. Sending out her own tweet to promote the stream, Ocasio-Cortez wrote, "Lastly, we wouldn't need to talk about bathrooms at all if we acted like adults, washed our hands + minded our own business instead of trying to clock others. Going by track record, I'd feel safer in a bathroom w/ a trans woman than a powerful male executive any day of the week. If you'd like to use this as a good moment to support the queer community, there's a charity twitch stream going on for @Mermaids_Gender: https://twitter.com/mermaids_gender/status/1087086256914395137?s=21 ..."

AOC then jumped on the feed, surprising H.bomberguy and giving him a real jolt of energy—and helping him raise more money. Weiner, *Splinter News*'s reporter, concluded, "It sure looks like the joke's on Lineham [transphobic writer], because H.bomberguy's quest to play Donkey Kong 64 to 101 percent completion has now raised more than $250,000 for Mermaids. And the stream isn't over yet. Shout out to AOC, the only good politician."[32]

Ocasio-Cortez knows that she has a special ability to shine a light on big problems facing vulnerable communities and has not shied away from using her spotlight

---

32   Ibid.

to help. Often, her efforts subject her to attacks from online harassers, but she persists. This generosity of spirit has won her many friends and impressed those who may not have otherwise given her the benefit of the doubt. Speaking out for fellow members of Congress who have been attacked for their policy views or appearance or religion as well as transkids and others, Ocasio-Cortez wields her social media sword as a defender of the weak and vulnerable and as a warrior for justice. But her sharpest tool is her wit and her wonder, her engaging tone and her engagement with her followers and her colleagues.

AOC may be entertaining, but part of that entertainment is pedagogical. She uses social media to educate the broader public about public policy, going deep into details but doing so in a way that is understandable and compelling. She doesn't leave it to her official website or wonky non-profits to explain the ins and outs of her policy proposals. In digestible bites, she lays out the arguments for her ideas and effectively counters those of her opponents. For example, embracing a robust progressive tax policy that includes raising tax rates on the wealthy, Ocasio-Cortez took to twitter to explain marginal tax rates (and also to eviscerate a critic). Former Wisconsin Governor Scott Walker thought he had her when he tweeted his support for tax cuts and his critique of AOC's position. "Explaining tax rates before Reagan to 5th graders: 'Imagine if you did chores for your grandma and she gave you $10. When you got home, your parents took $7 from you.' The students said: 'That's not fair!' Even 5th graders get it."[33] AOC was quick with her comeback: "Explaining marginal taxes to a far-right former Governor: Imagine if you did chores for abuela & she gave you $10. When you got home, you got to keep it, because it's only $10. Then we taxed the billionaire in town because he's making tons of money underpaying the townspeople."[34] Her effective, devastating, and cheeky response was a slam dunk to former Wisconsin Governor Scott Walker's effort to critique her ideas. Ocasio-Cortez had pulled the rug out under him with one tweet. Point for AOC.

And to talk to the public about climate change, AOC also took to social media. Fluent in Instagram as well as Twitter, Ocasio-Cortez speaks directly to people as she carries on her daily life. Reporter Vera Bergengruen, formerly of BuzzFeed, tweeted, "More than 8,000 people on Instagram are watching @AOC live stream herself putting together IKEA furniture, drinking wine and talking about the GOP and climate change."[35] She captured people's attention and then gave them real information about one of our most significant challenges. So many more people will tune into a conversation like that on social

33 Scott Walker, Twitter, January 15, 2019, https://twitter.com/ScottWalker/status/1085199713463422981.
34 Alexandria Ocasio-Cortez, Twitter, January 15, 2019, https://twitter.com/aoc/status/1085245511324581889?lang=en.
35 Vera Bergen, Twitter, January 15, 2019, https://twitter.com/VeraMBergen?lang=en.

media than might on traditional television or radio news. The impact of an educator like AOC can be enormous.

But she also recognizes how to use live events and offline educational opportunities to reach a broader audience—in part making those events exciting by illustrating complex ideas through understandable approaches. She famously expounded on the damaging and corrupting role of campaign money in American politics in a House hearing on H.R.1, a major bill to restore democracy, prompting social media influencer James Corden to tweet about a clip of AOC in committee, "Oh my god. This is just sensational. Please watch and retweet." One commentator even titled his piece on H.R.1, the multipronged reform bill introduced by House Democrats, "AOC is Making C-SPAN fun."[36] Making C-SPAN fun . . . and social media influencers tweeting about congressional committee hearings: that's how you engage the electorate in major policy debates.

Openly enjoying herself, Ocasio-Cortez uses new approaches to witness questioning both to get real answers out of those appearing before the committee but also to allow for real understanding of the issues under debate. Sitting on the important House Oversight and Government Reform Committee—a seat she had to fight for—she led witnesses through a "lightning-round game" where she made herself a "bad guy"—"which I'm sure

---

36 Branko Marcetic, "AOC is Making C-Span Fun," *The Jacobin*, accessed August 19, 2019, https://www.jacobinmag.com/ 2019/02/c-span-aoc-ocasio-cortez-hearings.

half the room would agree with anyway," she joked—who's trying to "get away with as much bad things as possible, ideally to enrich myself and advance my interests." *Jacobin Magazine*'s Branko Marcetic summed up her achievement. He noted that in a vanishingly brief period of time, AOC was able to convey several key concepts including how out in the open is the corruption of our political system ("you're going to help me legally get away with all of this"); how few protections we have against legislators being bought by corporate interests ("Is there any hard limit that I have in terms of what legislation I'm allowed to touch ... based on the special interest funds that I accepted?" "There's no limits"); the ease with which the president can be corrupted by people or organizations with money ("Every person in this body is being held to a higher ethical standard than the president of the United States"); and how her colleagues on the committee probably themselves had some taint of special interest ("We have these influences existing in this body, which means that these influences are here in this committee shaping the questions that are being asked of you all").

Marcetic concluded, "That she does it all through the medium of a classroom game and with a sense of fun makes the whole thing even more remarkable to watch."[37] He was truly right to underscore that one reason that the public turns away from politics is because they don't trust politicians and think the elected officials have forgotten

---

37 Ibid.

their constituents (remember Joe Crowley?). But the disconnect also comes from the fact that people are anesthetized by the dry way in which issues are discussed. There's more than a bit of "eat your peas," while voters crave some ice cream every once in a while. It was a hard-won victory to bring cameras into Congressional hearing rooms and on the floor of each house, but the content leaves a lot to be desired in terms of entertainment value. To combat a politician and manipulator like Donald Trump, the public needs someone to counter him by communicating in a way that attracts their interest as well. Marcetic understands that one part of the attraction of a Donald Trump, even though he is not aligned with some supporters on issues, is because he's entertaining, whereas someone who earns voters' respect, like Barack Obama, "was dull as chalk when he wasn't giving a major speech. Ocasio-Cortez has shown she can bring the style that's made her a force of nature on social media to a committee hearing and, more importantly, do it in a way that makes clear to the public just how easy it is for the rich—or 'bad guys,' to use her words—to control the political system."[38]

The left struggles to get people to pay attention to process issues, like voting and campaign finance, but they are foundational elements of our democracy. Too many times, well-intentioned policy advocates and elected officials drown their listeners in an outpouring of data and jargon, rather than illustrating how the problem affects their lives and undermines their futures. AOC can help

---

38 Ibid.

us communicate to the public about how the system is rigged against them and how to fix it, without overwhelming the audience with wonkery.

Ocasio-Cortez hasn't restricted her educational skills to policy matters nor her exuberance and charm. She's also found the joy in teaching her fellow House Democrats how to use social media, with all that that entails. In an engaging podcast with Ryan Grim and Briahna Gray of *The Intercept*, AOC explained the challenge of needing to balance her duties in Congress with just living her life, which requires a lot of multitasking to use her time both to cook or garden and talk to the public:

> **AOC:** So we have to figure out ways to kind of use the small pockets of time that we do have creatively, even if it's just when I'm, you know, prepping vegetables for dinner, if I can get, if I can get a conversation about policy in there, it's tremendously effective.
> **RG:** That might be like a 200-level or 300-level social media course that you taught.
> **AOC:** Yeah!

Grim inquired how AOC managed to teach her colleagues in Congress how to use social media, as he put it, "a kind of Twitter for Dummies." Ocasio-Cortez laughingly deflected the shade Grim threw on the House members, expressing enthusiasm for how much interest the other Democrats had in learning to be more adept in twenty-first-century communications tools. She was not alone in serving as a guru for the less Twitter adept. She described how she and "Ted Lieu, who himself has a very large Twitter following, Congresswoman Debbie Dingell as well as some of the Twitter government kind of outreach folks at, at Twitter itself" led the session. "[A]ctually," she continued, "House Ethics was there because there are House ethics rules based on what you can tweet, when you can tweet it, and so they kind of covered the ethics side. And I kind of covered just my approach and how we can better get, I think, a party message to really resonate with people."[39]

It's funny and sweet, and a recognition that she knows that she can't change the world alone. Her effectiveness as a legislator requires her partnering with other legislators at speaking to voters and getting them to turn out at election time. AOC can't fight the battle without fellow soldiers for justice—and they need to be armed with memes and GIFs to counter the forces of evil.

But Alexandria Ocasio-Cortez makes sure not to be all

---

39 Ryan Grim and Briahna Gray, "Podcast Special: Alexandria Ocasio-Cortez on her First Weeks in Washington," *The Intercept*, January 28, 2019, https://theintercept.com/2019/01/28/alexandria-ocasio-cortez-podcast/.

policy—or even all work—all the time. Remember the dancing video? Her springtime Twitter feed found joy in the growth of new plants, and focused some attention on her community garden. AOC tweeted on April 7, 2019, "Garden planting success! This is my first time trying a garden like this, so let's see how it goes. Shoshin approach. Big ups to Ginkgo Gardens for giving me lots of guidance this morning. Here is their helpful blog for beginners: https://www.ginkgogardens.com/blog."[40] Announcing her new gardening plans earlier that day, AOC seemed to be smiling through her tweet, calling out "Happy Sunday! Excited to say I'm tending to a community garden plot for the next few months :) It's a 4x4 plot we get to tend to now through Sept. Any greenthumbs out with sage words of advice? What should I plant? (Ideally at least 1 edible thing but we can do flowers too)."[41] Asking her followers to be collaborators and not just witnesses to her joy is another AOC trait.

Her garden is also a useful metaphor. It's a productive effort, giving back food and flowers; but community gardens do more than just provide sustenance for the body. They also help build strong social networks offline and a shared concern for the earth and a cleaner environment. So it's a metaphor for larger engagement, but it also provides something good in one's life from

40   Alexandria Ocasio-Cortez, Twitter, April 7, 2019, https://twitter.com/AOC/status/1115031113423052800

41   Alexandria Ocasio-Cortez, Twitter, April 7, 2019, https://twitter.com/aoc/status/1085245511324581889?lang=en.

food to friendship. A *Washington Post* journalist, Adrian Higgins, who writes about gardens in the Home section of the paper, was pleased to see her bring attention to the growing and nurturing of plants. When Higgins saw AOC's post on Twitter, he was ready to respond only to see many of her followers had already jumped in to participate in the discussion. "[B]efore I could fumble for my glasses and compose an answer," Higgins wrote, "she had received 8,300 responses. Even those helpful fans may have been too slow off the mark; she soon announced that she had gone to a Capitol Hill garden center and received sufficient guidance. The last post of the day showed the plot fully planted with an instant garden that included herbs, vegetables and blooms."[42]

Higgins was gratified, that not only did AOC get lots of advice for gardening but that gardening and related policy issues also got a boost through her star power. "Now, maybe I'm naive, and AOC is in three tweets cannily signaling her solidarity with a suite of partisan environmental and social issues, such as addressing urban food deserts and climate change. But aren't those issues lawmakers should be facing?" Higgins asked.[43] And he also noted that even if a small garden doesn't do a lot to address those bigger issues, it does an enormous amount

---

42   Adrian Higgins, "Alexandria Ocasio-Cortez Planted a Community Garden Plot. It's Good for the Earth – and Her," *Washington Post*, May 1, 2019, https://www.washingtonpost.com/lifestyle/home/aoc-plants-a-garden-and-the-twitterverse-pays-attention/2019/04/29/38c614fa-66b9-11e9-82ba-fcfeff232e8f_story.html?utm_term=.ae7037a650ad.
43   Ibid.

of good for the psyche as well as highlight local issues of adequate water, animal habitat, and cooling shade.

And as of July 2019, AOC's garden was thriving: "My community garden plot is doing well! I was nervous checking up on it today, because Congress has been out of session for 2 weeks for district work. I left it with a bunch of watering stakes/bottles and hoped for the best. They blew up! Peep the collard greens!"[44]

Ultimately, she pulled it off. In late spring of 2019, Ocasio-Cortez announced her first harvest: "This is a public announcement that we successfully grew, harvested, & ate spinach, collard greens, & swiss chard from the garden plot! As such, I now reserve the right to use this emoji." And she inserted a female farmer emoji, holding a pitchfork. One of her followers cheekily replied, "I see what you're up to miss AOC this is so you can go to the farmers of American [sic] and say I'm one of you vote for me for president. Political long game. I like it."[45]

Other members of Congress might be spending time after work or on weekends doing the power fund-raising tour, but it's nice to know that Ocasio-Cortez spends at least a little time with her collards. May your garden grow! And perhaps, just perhaps, she will endear herself to a few farmers along the way. We will have to wait and see.

44 Alexandria Ocasio-Cortez, Twitter, April 29, 2019, https:// twitter.com/AOC/status/1123031563715928065?ref.
45 Alexandria Ocasio-Cortez, Twitter, April 29, 2019, https:// twitter.com/AOC/status/1123031563715928065?ref.

★ ★ ★

AOC's dance video encapsulates the central point of AOC's impact—she shows young women how to embrace their own unique selves and their own eccentricity and to find that beautiful and not shameful. Jenny Hollander of *Marie Claire* found real pleasure in witnessing AOC's response to the right-wing effort to troll her over the video, writing "Anyway, because the internet always comes through, a new account called 'AOC Dances to Every Song' popped up on Twitter, which is...exactly what it sounds like. From Bowie to Prince to Darude to the Super Mario theme, AOC's now-legendary dance has been set to all sorts of music." She described the different emotions she felt based on the music that had been matched with the video, writing ". . . after listening to Toto's 'Africa' dubbed over it, I'm feeling all kinds of spiritual. . . . Now, if you'll excuse me, I'm off to dance to 'Africa' and pretend I have half the grace of AOC doing it."[46]

But Hollander missed a big part of the message—she set up a very stereotypical female dynamic of measuring herself against someone else who she thinks is more beautiful, more talented, taller, thinner, stronger, smarter, you name it, and then finding herself wanting ("and pretend I have half the grace of AOC doing it"). One thing we should learn from AOC is not to judge ourselves

---

46 Jenny Hollander, "Here's Alexandria Ocasio-Cortez Dancing to All of Your Favorite Songs," *Marie Claire*, January 4, 2019, https://www.marieclaire.com/politics/a25749419/alexandria-ocasio-cortez-dancing-twitter/.

that way, in comparison to others or even to judge ourselves for pure expressions of joy. Women tend to be
particularly hard on themselves, frequently engaging in
self-censorship, self-denial, and self-criticism. From an
early age, women are inundated with negative images—
women are either madonnas or whores, mothers or sluts,
or sometimes both—that have existed as a familiar trope
of literature, religion, and popular culture for eons. We
internalize these criticisms and fear to express ourselves
or to challenge others' views. We assume we don't have
"the grace" to speak out—or dance. If there's a lesson to
draw, it is indeed that we should all dance to our own
song—so long as that song is self-affirming and not other-
denying. Part of staying in the fight is not allowing
self-criticism to overwhelm our efforts to fight for justice.
Remember the flower garden; AOC is a role model for
self-care, something that couldn't be more necessary in
this day and age.

How do we learn to dance when we want to dance,
critics be damned? Dancing to your own music is hard
and first requires you to accept yourself, and even to like
yourself. While that seems easy and obvious, as Jenny
Hollander shows, it's not in fact so straightforward. So
many of us fight those inner voices that say that we don't
dance well enough to do it in public. The first step is to
recognize and name that inner critic. And shut her down.
Your inner voice should be your best friend, your ally,
and your cheerleader, telling you that you too can dance
in public. It means accepting and liking who you are.

That should not depend on what others think—women, especially, are too sensitive to the shaming that can come from social media, negative friends, or even family. Sometimes that means going along with friends' behavior that is unpleasant—like shaming others. Think "mean girls." Or drinking or partying to be in the popular social crowd despite preferring to see a movie or have a quiet dinner. At the end of the day, you have to decide what makes you happy and not try to be someone else. Like AOC, if you are true to yourself, you will respect yourself and others will as well. What self-respect produces is the recognition by others that you are true to your beliefs. Even if people don't agree with you, they will acknowledge that you are strong and that you are an individual who is unique and valuable. AOC is not conforming to others' views of how a young woman in America should behave. She's actually living out the familiar quote that "well-behaved women seldom make history." Well that's true. That's because "behaving" usually means "conforming," and conforming means not being your own true self. As Rita Mae Brown wrote, "The reward for conformity is that everyone likes you except yourself." Nonconforming is an act of bravery and difficult—but the impact is decisive. It allows us to be our best, when we are living out our true nature and acting on our beliefs. It's not easy, but it's a better path than the one of good behavior, conformity, and self-denial.

In an interview in *HipLatina*, Ocasio-Cortez explained why she needed to take time for some self-care after a whirlwind campaign and a strenuous adjustment to life as a congresswoman. Just as important she related why she found it important to make that public. "I keep things raw and honest here with you all since I believe public servants do a disservice to our communities by pretending to be perfect. It makes things harder for others who aspire to run someday if they think they have to be superhuman before they try," said AOC. "No one in Congress is superhuman—I've seen it myself. A lot of campaigns are based on telling a 'superhuman' story and I respectfully disagree with that tactic, although many people ARE inspiring. You don't have to be perfect, but you have to be 100% committed."[47]

What matters is being true to yourself so you can act on your beliefs. Liking and respecting yourself are the first steps to achieve that. But so is giving yourself some time to take care of your own needs. That doesn't mean just "having a big glass of red wine in your living room like Olivia Pope from *Scandal*" or even mani-pedis or spa vacations. It's a lifestyle, not a moment. The project of self-care, *HipLatina* is right to note, "is only effective when it becomes a daily practice and it can be as simple as putting yourself first, making time for yourself to decompress, resting, exercising, meditating, or practice mindfulness. It's about taking a deep breath, silencing the noise and chaos around you, closing off distractions,

---

47 "Alexandria Ocasio-Cortez Gets Real About Taking Time Off for Self-Care Being a WOC," *HipLatina*, December 18, 2018, https:// hiplatina.com/alexandria-ocasio-cortez-self-care-time-off/.

and paying close attention to how your body feels and your mind and inner emotions feel."[48]

We all hope that our lives will be a marathon and not a sprint—that's certainly true for Alexandria Ocasio-Cortez, who has only begun her time in public service. She's already facing the ire of conservatives and even some Democratic Party elements who may mount a primary challenge when AOC runs for reelection in 2020. Being true to oneself also means being true to one's politics and values. For AOC fans, that means an expectation that her singular voice that has been calling out truth to power since she began her run for office will continue to be loud and inspiring. What has made her stand out among politicians is her clear authentic commitment to values and the policy proposals they lead her to embrace. "A breath of fresh air" is a clichéd phrase, but it helps capture her impact on the public.

From my perspective, a role model like AOC is so needed. I wish I had had one when I was younger. As a little girl, I was fierce, not afraid to get dirty, loved climbing trees and playing baseball, ran barefoot through the neighborhood (and occasionally stepped on glass). But as the subtle remarks started to register with me— friends' mothers commenting that I was a "tomboy" (by the way, what a terrible term!), that I was always in pants and my hair was a mess, that I wasn't quite right somehow—I began to lose my fierceness. From a child oblivious to the rules that say that little girls should wear

---

48 Ibid.

pink, play quietly, and be pretty, I began to hold back. But in sports, I found a niche and friends, and I began to question my self-questioning. And with that small beginning, I began to reclaim myself. It is a hard process to trust one's own impulses, and it requires bravery to act on them. It's not a single victory, but a process of small achievements won through taking risks, challenging oneself, and recognizing that even when others may throw shade, it's a strengthening process and one that results in greater happiness. French poet Guillaume Apollinaire wisely wrote, "Now and then it's good to pause in our pursuit of happiness and just be happy."

I have never regained the oblivious freedom from the conformity police I had as a small child, but I have become better able to shut them down. The E. E. Cummings quote from the beginning of the chapter is my mantra: "It takes courage to grow up and turn out to be who you really are." Alexandria Ocasio-Cortez can help all of us find our own courage. True not only for little girls, your comfort in your own body and brain is especially empowering. Let's all dance to our own music.

CHAPTER TWO
Take Me Seriously

"OH, ANYBODY RANKED ABOUT A hundred could beat the women's champion . . . Hell, I could beat Billie Jean!" tennis player Bobby Riggs once said, prior to his Battle of the Sexes with Billie Jean King.[49]

"After [I won], he jumped the net and said, 'I underestimated you.' I couldn't believe it," King said. "Respect always wins, because you can put your head on your pillow at night and know you did the right thing."[50]

---

49 Tim Grierson, "Was Bobby Riggs a Sexist? An Opportunist? Or Just Misunderstood?," *Mel Magazine*, accessed August 16, 2019, https://melmagazine.com/en-us/story/was-bobby-riggs-a-sexist-an-opportunist-or-just-misunderstood.

50 Anna Klassen, "The Real Reason Billie Jean King Beat Bobby Riggs Has Nothing to do with Tennis," *Bustle*, September 22, 2017, https://www.bustle.com/p/the-real-reason-billie-jean-king-beat-bobby-riggs-has-nothing-to-do-with-tennis-2375744.

When President Donald Trump attacked Alexandria Ocasio-Cortez on her bold new plan for a Green New Deal for climate change, dismissively calling it a program "done by a young bartender," AOC told *Newsweek* that the "last guy who underestimated me lost." "That's all I gotta say about that," she added.[51]

For women, being underestimated is an ongoing challenge, to put it mildly. We are constantly undervalued and undermined, ignored and overlooked, dismissed and disparaged, but when we try to speak up for ourselves, to share our ideas, to be part of the conversation, we are deemed "aggressive" or lacking in "team working skills." I know so many women who have faced this criticism—you are a mouse or a bitch, a wallflower or a diva. Somehow, it's impossible to be a smart, strong woman without the backbiting and put-downs of those who feel threatened. There are whispers and outright insults, direct snubs, and the indirect hurt of being ignored and excluded. But continue on we must, taking on the criticism of being outspoken or having opinions—yes, we dare!—and ultimately we prove our value and our worth. And either our challengers learn their lesson . . . or they lose.

The young congresswoman from the Bronx, Alexandria Ocasio-Cortez, could not better exemplify

---

51 Ramsey Touchberry, "Alexandria Ocasio-Cortez Warns Donald Trump: 'The Last Guy Who Underestimated Me Lost,'" *Newsweek,* April 3, 2019, https://www.newsweek.com/alexandria-ocasio-cortez-donald-trump-1385244.

this paradigm. She is a lightning rod for misogynistic and racist Internet trolls but also the subject of condescension from some elements of the media and mainstream elites. Attacked and underestimated, critiqued endlessly for having opinions and speaking out (imagine what would be said about a congressman who didn't have opinions), for her clothes, and for her friends, AOC nonetheless "persisted"—and persists. Senator Elizabeth Warren, who wrote about Ocasio-Cortez for *Time*'s 100 most influential people issue, clearly finds her a young and inspiring model for the women who keep going despite the headwinds of criticism and condescension. AOC's—and Warren's—challenge is one that is endemic to womanhood, and her success can teach us a lot about how to use the gale-force winds to fill our sails rather than push us back. How can we face down the patronizing attitude of the patriarchy in the moment but also what can we do to tear it down in the long term? Those are the lessons we need to learn.

Don't forget that in their one congressional debate, Congressman Joe Crowley could not even be bothered to show up to face Alexandria Ocasio-Cortez. Instead, he sent a former New York City Council member, Annabel Palma, to stand in his place to face AOC, someone Crowley apparently discounted as a nonentity. We know how that turned out. She got 57.13 percent of the vote (15,897)

to his 42.5 percent (11,761), winning by nearly fifteen points. No one had expected her to win. In a June 27 piece, *Time* proclaimed her victory "the biggest upset of the 2018 [primary] elections so far."[52] And the *New York Times* wrote that Crowley's loss was "the most significant loss for a Democratic incumbent in more than a decade, and one that will reverberate across the party and the country."[53] It was truly shocking for a member of Congress in a "safe seat" to get sent packing, especially by someone so young and inexperienced—and so decisively. But that's what AOC did, and that despite the fact that she was outspent by a margin of eighteen to one. That was a lot of spending against her, most of which came in the end of the campaign, when Crowley finally woke up to the seriousness of the fight. But even after pouring in money, he could not put out the flames that were burning down his candidacy.

Joe Crowley, the incumbent targeted by AOC, lost his reelection in large part because he had ignored the district as it changed both in complexion and in political orientation. Attracted to possible national leadership in the Democratic Party, the congressman tried to build his profile on a bigger stage than the Bronx and Queens.

---

52   Phillip Elliott, "How Alexandria Ocasio-Cortez Pulled Off the Biggest Upset of 2018," *Time*, June 27, 2018, https://time.com/5322905/joe-crowley-alexandria-ocasio-cortez/.

53   Shane Goldmacher and Jonathan Martin, "Alexandria Ocasio-Cortez Defeats Joseph Crowley in Major Democratic House Upset, *New York Times*, June 26, 2018, https://www.nytimes.com/2018/06/26/nyregion/joseph-crowley-ocasio-cortez-democratic-primary.html.

Raising money from Wall Street for other Democrats, campaigning among centrist candidates and handing them cash, Crowley had his eyes on another prize (and on defeating another woman). His goal was to replace Nancy Pelosi as Speaker after the 2018 election should Democrats regain the House. His politicking among Wall Street donors and conservative Democrats took him away from New York and his district. Crowley took his eye off the ball. And it hit him in the face.

AOC did not blink. She kept her focus firmly on the race and why she deserved the votes of the constituents of New York's fourteenth congressional district. Unlike the absent congressman, she knew she had to be prepared for the challenge. She stayed in the district. She worked hard to speak to her future constituents. And she ran a smart campaign that took advantage of the changing demographics of the district, recognized that the voters were more progressive than Crowley, and embraced social media and alternative news sources to spread her message to new and occasional voters. Indeed, she knew that she could have a particular appeal to younger voters and voters of color, particularly Latinx voters, and that gave her candidacy the momentum of change in an election when change was in the air. But the bottom line is that Ocasio-Cortez knew that this race was not something she could take for granted. But she also knew that if she worked hard, she could prevail, despite being underestimated consistently by the Democratic Party and by pundits.

Of great importance was her sophisticated approach to use of new technologies to bring out new and younger voters. Responding to sources like Twitter and Instagram rather than the *New York Times* or the *New York Post*, these potential voters found her voice compelling and fresh—she spoke to them in a way Crowley not only could not speak but didn't even appear to try to speak. Her issues were clear: get rid of the US Immigration and Customs Enforcement (ICE) and pass Medicare for All. She made sure to speak to reporters from newer online media outlets like *The Intercept*, *HuffPost*, and *Refinery29*. And while she did go the traditional route by using some radio advertising in the campaign, her main focus was on digital platforms—those ads can go viral, while radio and TV don't have the same reach. And of course, sophisticated users of social media know that a viral post or tweet can migrate to mainstream platforms, the medium becoming the substance. With thousands of shares, her tweets started to penetrate to a broader audience and become news. Though the traditional media didn't cover her as a "serious" candidate, she did start to get attention.

But nothing can be taken in isolation. According to Corbin Trent, who served as communications director for her campaign and then for her congressional office, AOC won for many, synergistic reasons: the nonstop voter contact through door-to-door canvassing, getting trusted voices to speak out in her support, and generating positive attention in the media through a variety of approaches, including Twitter and Instagram. "There was an element of luck here, right?" said Trent to *City & State New York.* Trent pointed to the "co-endorsement" made by progressive Democratic House member Representative Ro Khanna, who changed his original Crowley pick to bless them both—in translation, that was really an endorsement of Ocasio-Cortez with a little tiny bit of hedging for Crowley. Similarly, actress Cynthia Nixon, who was running for governor, also embraced AOC after initially giving her support to Crowley. "If Ro Khanna hadn't done what he did the way he did it, no way would that have got the attention it got. The fact that the endorsement from Cynthia Nixon came when it did, the fact that she delayed it till the day before the primary," all serendipitously contributed to her win, Trent said.

Underestimating AOC was lethal for Crowley's campaign. Crowley's apparent lack of interest in her challenge and his unwillingness to treat her as serious candidate ultimately carried over to the press. With Crowley treating her like a nonentity, reporters wrote stories that played up her youth or novelty, making her into a unicorn and not a lion. A member of the Crowley campaign remarked that "There was a general unwillingness of [the media] to write anything other than the Cinderella upset story as opposed to those things that would potentially disqualify her," the source said, adding that even members of the press "didn't take her seriously." But once she won, even the Crowley campaign staff person acknowledged she had won because of her ideas and her hard work. "Look, it's a credit to her. She did a very good job of organizing and in generating a turnout spike among younger voters," the aide told the news site *City & State New York*.

AOC worked her district hard. For over a year, she had been doing the old-fashioned campaign work of door knocking, talking to her neighbors and future constituents but also treading the new pathways opened up by the Internet. Fluent in social media, she aggressively communicated on Twitter and other outlets, building a base of online support much more visible to her targeted voters than the older symbols of a strong campaign, yard signs and bumper stickers. "Everybody keeps saying 'digital is the future of campaigns.' It's not the future of campaigns, it's the present of campaigns," said Trent. Again, though, none of this happened in isolation. While she may have put a lot of effort into the digital side of the campaign, those tactics also reinforced the direct voter contact. She did her door knocking at the same time she reached out via social media. "What we did is load this 75,000 somewhat-likely primary voters into our digital marketing tools and we hit those folks with ads fairly frequently," Trent said. "Then we knocked on their doors, we sent them mail, we knocked on their doors again, we called them." She was speaking to people who hadn't heard from Crowley in a long time or ever. Living in Virginia, rarely coming back to Queens, let alone the Bronx, hanging out with bankers at fancy cocktail parties, Crowley was an alien in his own district. AOC, by contrast, excited people who were frightened by politics as usual in the age of Trump and reached people who didn't think politicians cared about their concerns and daily challenges.

While recognizing that the election was a wave election for progressive candidates, and nowhere more so than in New York, where several incumbents lost reelection, reporter Grace Segers agreed that the biggest reason for AOC's victory was AOC. "Ocasio-Cortez's victory may be the result of a confluence of events and a knack for strategy, but it also speaks to the candidate herself, and her ability to harness the undercurrent of enthusiasm that has been brewing in the Democratic Party since the 2016 presidential primary between Hillary Clinton and Bernie Sanders."[54] One element that clearly helped her was the recognition by some political organizers that the Democrats needed to recruit new blood, outside of the usual suspects—young progressives of color. Corbin Trent, who had originally come to AOC from the Justice Democrats organization, said that the "biggest shared goal" of Justice Democrats and a similar entity, Brand New Congress, was "removing the corrupting influence of money in politics." According to Trent, the two groups work together to ensure that nontraditional candidates are not shut out of the system and can run without depending on special interests and corporate financing. "Right now our Congress is 81 percent men," Trent said. "It's mostly white men, it's mostly millionaires, it's

---

54 Grace Segers, "How Alexandria Ocasio-Cortez won the race that shocked the country," *City and State New York*, June 27, 2018, https:// www.cityandstateny.com/articles/politics/campaigns-elections/ how-alexandria-ocasio-cortez-won-race-shocked-country.html.

mostly lawyers."[55] And just as Crowley underestimated AOC, so typically do these corporate executives, bankers, and lawyers underestimate women generally.

AOC created a new formula for campaigns that builds on the tools of the past and amplifies them through social media. She was thorough, hard-working, and methodical. Those who believe she won simply because Crowley was out of step with his district seriously miss the mark. Not only were her hard work and creative use of new communications tools decisive parts of her victory, but this approach also set her up to be a force as a freshman House member. Unlike most newly elected members of Congress, Ocasio-Cortez arrived with a constituency that was fully engaged in her efforts to change the crony culture she found among Democrats that had been embodied by Joe Crowley. A dragon-slayer, she had brought down a formidable party leader and rainmaker. And she was ready to continue to fight in Washington, DC, much to the chagrin of senior Democrats who expect newcomers to sit in the back and stay quiet. That is not really the AOC way.

And she continues to work hard in her district. She knows that she won because people put their faith in her to help make things better for them. So she pays attention. *Time* reporter Charlotte Alter tagged along with her in her district, describing the seriousness and attention that AOC

---

55   Manohla Dargis, "'Knock Down the House' Review: Running to Win Hearts and Minds and Votes," April 30, 2019, *New York Times,* https://www.nytimes.com/2019/04/30/movies/knock-down-the-house-review.html.

gives to her neighbors back in New York. "When she goes to meetings in her district, Ocasio-Cortez takes notes, hunched over a single-subject notebook as if she were in science class," wrote Alter. "As soon as she starts speaking, the room changes. In a hot and stuffy education meeting in the Queens neighborhood of Jackson Heights, the crowd stood up and cheered when she took the microphone, then swarmed her afterward to ask for hugs and selfies." Alter described the community board meeting at a wedding hall in Astoria, Queens, where one elderly attendee napped the entire time but did wake up to snap a few photos of AOC with his phone. AOC stuck around "to listen to a constituent's concerns about the rise of anti-Semitism. Her beige heels, slightly scuffed, were a half size too big."[56] Many members of Congress would have worried that their appearance needs to be perfect and coifed—so many of them visit dermatologists and beauty consultants for tucks and tanning. AOC just wanted to hear from her constituents so she could go back to Washington with a better understanding of the challenges they face in this economy, in the job market, with health care, with education and child care.

When she's in Washington, DC, she also works hard. In fact, many congressional staff members have commented that she attends more hearings than her colleagues. She pays attention and comes prepared. A workhorse, not

---

56 Charlotte Alter, "'Change Is Closer Than We Think.' Inside Alexandria Ocasio-Cortez's Unlikely Rise," *Time,* March 21, 2019, http://time.com/longform/alexandria-ocasio-cortez-profile/.

a show pony, is the consensus.[57] Particularly for younger people, especially women and people of color, it is a given that they will be underestimated and that means they have to prove constantly that they are talented—that they deserve to be at the table. It's a day in, day out process of showing value and can be exhausting. That's what AOC has done over and over, consistently outhustling and outperforming her critics. From her campaign against Joe Crowley to the congressional hearing on campaign finance and ethics reform to the oversight hearing featuring Trump's fixer Michael Cohen, AOC showed those who would call her a lightweight and short-termer that she's serious and smart—in fact, smarter than they are. She brought to her work on the Hill the same work ethic she showed on her campaign, a work ethic, by the way, that low-wage workers, like the bartender and waiter she had been, must demonstrate every day to keep their jobs. She knows that hearings are theater and that like any piece of acting, one must prepare, learn one's lines, and understand the audience and the goal of the drama. Many members of Congress forget the narrative arc that makes the difference between a hearing that is valuable and one that is a waste of time. They approach it by thinking only of how to make a flowery or fiery speech without thinking through how they will help their colleagues or use witness testimony to illustrate a policy objective. But if we remember why hearings are held, we know that it is of vital importance to have a strategy. Hearings are the process of proving a point, just

---

57   Ibid.

like in the courtroom. Each witness must be questioned so as to lay out evidence in support of the greater argument, to advance a point of view, a piece of legislation, or a prosecution. It requires discipline and self-control to do the hard work of laying the foundation for each additional question, building an edifice brick by brick. The self-control means not giving in to impulses to grandstand and give speeches instead of putting the witness and the questions first. But that's what wins the hearing. AOC had imbibed the lesson that hard work and preparation can win the day—and prove doubters wrong.

Early in her first year in Congress, Ocasio-Cortez showed her brainpower—and her self-discipline—in the hearing on the Democrats' top priority for 2019, the anti-corruption bill, H.R.1, otherwise known as the For the People Act. The bill addresses campaign finance reform but also voter suppression and ethics violations, seeking to expand and protect democracy in times of great challenge. All of these issues are complex and detailed, but the bill speaks to the widely held belief—that propelled Democrats into the House leadership—that Washington is broken and that Trump is making it worse. AOC used the hearing in her committee to address the campaign finance laws and lax enforcement that allow fat cats in Washington to buy politicians and for politicians to avoid being held accountable by their voters—or, as AOC put it in the hearing, they make it "super legal" for a lawmaker to be a "pretty bad guy." But she didn't leave it at that. She led witnesses through a set of questions that made it clear just how broken the system is. And in so doing, her acute questioning prompted *NowThis News* to put out a video that quickly went viral, with a clip of Ocasio-Cortez playing a "lightning round" game with those who had come to testify. Through this "game," AOC illustrated how politicians can come very close to accepting direct bribes and it is all perfectly legal. She also remarked that the rules that apply to Congress are stricter than those that apply to the president.

"I'm going to be the bad guy, which, I'm sure, half the room would agree with anyway, and I want to get away with as much bad things as possible, ideally to enrich myself and advance my interests, even if that means putting my interests ahead of the American people," explained Ocasio-Cortez as she began her questioning during the hearing. "I have enlisted all of you as my co-conspirators, so you're going to help me legally get away with all of this." She ran through a set of questions: "Can she run a campaign entirely funded by corporate political action committees? Yes. Can she use that money to make hush payments and pay people off to get elected? Yes. Once in office, can she influence and write laws that might affect the groups from which she's taken special interest money? Yes. And can she hold stocks in companies the legislation she's writing might boost? Yes."[58]

---

58   Emily Stewart, "Alexandria Ocasio-Cortez's 'lightning round' on money in politics goes viral," *Vox,* February 8, 2019, https://www. vox.com/policy-and-politics/2019/2/8/18216884/alexandria-ocasio-cortez-video-campaign-finance.

After *NowThis* put out the video of AOC's questioning, over thirteen million viewers watched it—and learned from it. She took a topic not well understood by many people, and made it clear why they were right to have a visceral suspicion of politicians. They were right to think that the system is rigged, and she showed exactly in what way it is rigged. Most people feel that somehow candidates and elected officials are getting away with something, that the system is corrupt, but they don't necessarily understand exactly how and why that is true. AOC took them step by step through the legal ways corruption happens in Washington.

Most Americans agree that wealthy individuals and special interests shouldn't have an unlimited ability to influence politicians through campaign contributions. Beyond that intuition, however, people don't really know how the system works. AOC broke it down, spelling out how money for campaigns turns into access on the Hill, which turns into provisions in legislation and special treatment for those same donors. She described how an energy lobbyist who is seeking to protect fracking can give a member of Congress a check at an event before an election and then help shape the bills introduced by that same member of Congress. It sure looks like bribery.[59]

With her ability to draw out witnesses, getting them to admit that they take advantage of "access" to write laws that benefit their own bottom lines, Ocasio-Cortez provided a reality show of how Congress operates. Something

59   Ibid.

the public suspected has been acted out in a hearing and, because AOC knows how to script her performance, the show was compelling and became a must-watch video that educated thousands and thousands of Americans. The lobbyists didn't expect that. Once again, she had been underestimated, with consequences for those who didn't take her seriously. But she didn't just analyze the problem. With her colleagues, she laid out a plan to fix the broken system. AOC knows that just pointing out the failures of our democracy doesn't help anyone pay the rent—and certainly doesn't get them to vote. So she paired her critique with a remedy, H.R. 1, that would address each of the points she raised and brought to life in her questioning: how to get money out of politics, how to protect the right to vote, and how to enforce ethics in government.

She has brought a similar pedagogical approach to the climate crisis, educating obtuse conservative colleagues—but more importantly, the public—about the connection between poverty and environmental issues. Republican Sean Duffy, representing Wisconsin, tried to show that efforts to address climate change have the unintended consequence of raising the cost of basic needs like housing. Thinking he had discovered a weak spot in the Green New Deal, Duffy proclaimed "I think it's rich that we talk about how we care about the poor, but all the while we'll sign on to bills that dramatically increase the cost of a family to get into a home." (In actuality, the Green New Deal aims to address climate change broadly, not just by weatherizing buildings and incentivizing easy fixes like better light bulbs and insulation, but also through efforts to protect good jobs.[60]) But Duffy continued, thinking he had AOC trapped by his brilliant argumentation. "I don't think we should not focus on the rich, wealthy elites who will look at this and go, 'I love it, because I've got big money in the bank; everyone should do this. We should all sign onto it,'" Duffy said. "But if you're a poor family, just trying to make ends meet, it's a horrible idea."

"It's kind of like saying, 'I'll sign on to the Green New Deal, but I'll take a private jet from DC to California,'" he continued. "A private jet! Or 'I'll take my Uber SUV, I won't take the train.' Or 'I'll go to Davos, and I'll fly my private jet.' The hypocrisy!"

Alexandria Ocasio-Cortez is used to this kind of self-congratulatory stance by those who underestimate her. So many of us have faced these kind of smug interlocutors, but AOC was able to expose Duffy's flaws. Asked by Congresswoman Maxine Waters, the chairperson of the House Financial Services Committee that was holding the hearing, if she wanted to respond, Ocasio-Cortez turned to Duffy—and tore down his argument.

"I am very encouraged by the sudden concern on the other side of the aisle about climate change, and it makes

60   Philip Bump, "Ocasio-Cortez's Righteous—and Accurate—Anger about Poverty and the Environment," *Washington Post*, March 27, 2019,   https://www.washingtonpost.com/politics/2019/03/27/ocasio-cortezs-righteous-accurate-anger-about-poverty-environment/?utm_term=.2d565acd49c5.

me feel as though our efforts have been effective at the very least in distancing between the dangerous strategy of climate denial, which we know is costing us lives— at least 3,000 in Puerto Rico in Hurricane Maria," said Ocasio-Cortez. She went on to explain to Duffy that a degraded environment harms people regardless of their class—indeed the poor were more likely to suffer from climate change impacts. "You want to tell people that their concern and their desire for clean air and clean water is elitist? Tell that to the kids in the South Bronx which are suffering from the highest rates of childhood asthma in the country," she said. "Tell that to the families in Flint whose kids have—their blood is ascending in lead levels. Their brains are damaged for the rest of their lives. Call them elitist. You're telling them that those kids are trying to get on a plane to Davos? People are dying. They are dying. And the response across the other side of the aisle is to introduce an amendment five minutes before a hearing in a markup?" she went on. "This is serious. This should not be a partisan issue. This is about our constituents and all of our lives. Iowa, Nebraska, broad swaths of the Midwest are drowning right now. Underwater. Farms, towns that will never be recovered and never come back."

AOC made the connection between the climate crisis and the economic inequality she has also identified as a major threat to America, saying "If we tell the American public that we are more willing to invest and bail out big banks than we are willing to invest in our farmers and our urban families, then I don't know what we're here doing. I don't know what we're here doing." These communities, both rural and urban, that are economically stressed are subject to worse outcomes from both pollution and climate change.

AOC had had direct experience regarding the connection between financial and environmental stresses, having been singularly affected during her trip to the Standing Rock reservation, where she had participated in protests against the pipeline, and when she stopped to visit Flint, Michigan, on the way to North Dakota. Moreover, the floods that had happened in the Midwest around the time of the hearing had caused widespread damage and were a result, most likely, of climate change. The flooding also caused more pollution as wells and other water sources were tainted by the inundation.

As AOC explained to Duffy, "This is about our lives. This is about American lives, and it should not be partisan. Science should not be partisan." But would Duffy listen? No, not to her and not on climate change. Others were paying attention, though, in the public, for whom the exchange helped illuminate how climate change harms low-income communities and how fraudulent are the arguments of those like Duffy who try to convince these communities that safe drinking water is an "elite" issue.

Similarly, colleagues have criticized AOC for making the connection between the border crisis—that is, mass migration—and climate issues. People are leaving their countries, she's said, in part because they can't grow crops and have no water, jobs are drying up along with rivers and lakes, and children's health is suffering. Fox News trumpeted that Republicans in the House had called the linkage "ridiculous." Congressman Dan Crenshaw, who represents Texas, told Fox, "It's news to me, I didn't know the Green New Deal would also solve the border crisis. It's pretty clear that [Democrats are] not taking this seriously at all. I mean, listen, the numbers speak for themselves. This is not due to climate change," Crenshaw continued. "You know they've come to this point where they want to blame climate change for quite literally everything now, and sorry, but the Green New Deal is not going to solve that."[61]

Despite the naysayers, AOC, in her work on Capitol Hill and in explaining the Green New Deal, makes sure people understand that the connection between poverty, racism, and environmental degradation applies to the United States as well as abroad. As she experienced in her travel to Flint, Michigan, and in joining the protest against the pipeline in North Dakota, marginal communities bear the brunt of pollution and increasing temperatures. Many other experts have weighed in, from former Vice President Al Gore, an expert on climate change, and scholars like Michael Doyle. Says Doyle, an international

---

61   Victor Garcia, "Ocasio-Cortez's Linkage of Climate Change and Border Situation 'Ridiculous,' Crenshaw says," *Fox News*, April 10, 2019, https://www.foxnews.com/politics/aocs-linkage-of-climate-change-and-border-situation-ridiculous-crenshaw-says.

relations professor at Columbia University in New York, "If your farm has been dried to a crisp or your home has been inundated with water and you're fleeing for your life, you're not much different from any other refugee. The problem is that other refugees fleeing war qualify for that status, while you don't."[62]

Just because AOC's logic is supported by experts does not mean the underestimation ends there. So many women face it—it's a part of our daily existence like brushing our teeth or washing our hands. But some women have used the negative energy as a spur to do even better, to show those "underestimators" how wrong they really are.

Leslie Feinzaig, founder and CEO of the Female Founders Alliance, which brings together high-growth start-up founders and CEOs, described the moment when she decided to challenge those who doubted her abilities, saying "You know what? Watch me. Just watch me." Fenzaig said that was a spark for her when she decided to grab on to opportunities instead of doubting herself. The only way to show that you are capable is to do the job. Feinzaig continued, "You might underestimate me, but I believe that I can do this, and I'm just going to

62 Oliver Milman, Emily Holden, and David Agren, "The unseen driver behind the migrant caravan: climate change," *The Guardian*, October 30, 2018, https://www.theguardian.com/world/2018/oct/30/migrant-caravan-causes-climate-change-central-america.

keep going. It is such an indicator of future success."[63] The moment for me was in my mid-thirties. Working as Deputy Chief of Staff to US Senator Tom Daschle of South Dakota, I was helping find candidates for staff in other offices, including the newly elected senator from Washington, Maria Cantwell, who needed a chief of staff. I passed on several résumés, and then thought, *why not me?*

So after sharing lots of résumés with Cantwell's temporary aide, I decided to jump in. I knew I wasn't prepared, but when has that ever stopped a guy? I knew I could learn. And I did. Cantwell was elected in 2000. Many people remember that there was a disputed election that year . . . one that the Supreme Court decided for George W. Bush and against Al Gore. But fewer people recall that Washington State too had a recount and a close race. Maria Cantwell was finally declared the winner in mid-December. That meant that I was hired long after other Senate offices had fully staffed up. And I had to keep working on a big project for Senator Daschle even while beginning my job as Cantwell's chief of staff. It was insane. I took advantage of all the advice I could get from other Democratic chiefs of staff (the women were especially helpful, although not only women) and the Congressional Management Foundation. As a result,

---

63 Gwen Moran, "How Being Underestimated Made these Women More Successful," Fast Company, October 29, 2018, https://www.fastcompany.com/90254838/how-being-underestimated-made-these-women-more-successful.

I was able to help Cantwell get through an enormous backlog of mail and emails, assisted her in fund-raising her way out of a deep hole of debt, and ensured she had a robust and defensible policy platform. It was also the year of the September 11 attacks that threw our entire government into turmoil. We faced an overwhelming challenge of dealing with the response to terrorism, including debating the Patriot Act, economic dislocation in New York, and military retaliation against Afghanistan where the terrorists had been based. In addition, our office was closed because of an anthrax attack on the Hart Senate Office Building, so we had to work out of a temporary space that was not nearly big enough for everyone in Cantwell's employ. Oh, did I mention that there was a major earthquake in Washington State, and the senator's focus (and that of her staff) was needed to ensure that the Federal Emergency Management Agency was on the ground immediately and taking care of the needs of the residents who were suffering?

We got through it all, and Cantwell has now been reelected several times. I know I was an important part of her success, but it was a scary time. But if I had not taken on that challenge, I never would have learned all that I am capable of. I learned to lead, to manage, to negotiate, to facilitate, indeed all sorts of skills that have been deeply important to my work since that time. For once, I had not talked myself out of something difficult because I was afraid I might fail. But it did take a lot of focus, preparation, and collaboration—you can't usually prove doubters wrong if you don't roll up your sleeves and do your homework.

For me, and for other women, AOC is so compelling because she did not shy away from taking on a challenge many thought she wasn't ready for. And sometimes, like any person, she makes a mistake. But when she does, she picks herself up and moves on. She recognizes that it doesn't mean she is not up to the job. That's why she presses on, showing that she's a force to be reckoned with and anyone who thinks otherwise will soon see the truth. Many had not expected her to be so capable and smart in her work on Capitol Hill and especially in the high-stakes committee hearings involving the investigations into President Donald Trump and his campaign's involvement with Russia. In the House Oversight hearing at which Donald Trump's lawyer Michael Cohen testified, she asked him whether Trump had ever inflated property values for bank or insurance purposes and probed him for additional sources for information on how Trump had done so. As I wrote in my *New York Times* op-ed, "How Alexandria Ocasio-Cortez Won the Cohen Hearing," "She asked one question at a time, avoided long-winded speeches on why she was asking the question, and listened carefully to his answer, which gave her the basis for a follow-up inquiry. As a result, Mr. Cohen gave specific answers about Mr. Trump's shady practices, along with a road map for how to find out more. . . . In just five minutes, Ms. Ocasio-Cortez actually helped him lay out the facts to substantiate those charges." But this didn't happen just because she's smart; she also worked hard to prepare. Spending hours with her staff and committee staff, AOC made sure she knew how best to get evidence out of Cohen.

My piece went viral. Around one and a half million viewers read the piece and many of them commented on it. They shared it on Twitter. Most of the comments on Twitter and on the *New York Times*'s website commented on AOC with similar sentiments of admiration. She did an amazing job of laying a foundation for further investigation. But what I had also remarked on was how few members of Congress use hearings as effectively and, unfortunately, in that very hearing too few of her colleagues followed AOC's lead.

While many members of Congress seemed to want to make an *impression* with an impassioned speech that chewed up much of their question time, Alexandria Ocasio-Cortez wanted to make a *difference*. And she did.

In the summer of 2019, Congressman Andy Barr of Kentucky snidely tweeted out a letter he had sent to AOC, demanding an apology from her for having criticized his Republican colleague Dan Crenshaw for his attack on Congresswoman Ilhan Omar. Congresswoman Omar, in saying that many Muslims in America had been unfairly lumped in with the 9/11 terrorists and were suffering civil rights violations, was called a terrorism sympathizer by Republicans. AOC rose to her defense, prompting the ire of GOP members like Barr. Tweeted Barr, "Today, I delivered the letter below to @AOC, calling on her to apologize for her comments to our colleague @DanCrenshawTX before she plans her trip to Kentucky to learn how the Green New Deal could impact our Commonwealth."[64] Ron Klain tweeted the following in response:

> Also, @AoC, I'd like you to get the slippers from the Wicked Witch of the West before you come to Kentucky. And clean the Augean stables in a day. And solve this 64 x 64 rubics cube in under 2 minutes. But sure, I absolutely want you to come."[65]

Klain used his sarcasm to make clear how the right's dismissive underestimation has now turned to fear and contempt. Not sure that's an improvement exactly, but I don't think they will underestimate her any longer.

AOC's impact and political power have not been fleeting, as many had suspected they would be. In fact, she has enabled other women and allies to enter and win races for elected office, defying the odds, in part, because Ocasio-Cortez spoke out on their behalf. In June 2019, Tiffan Caban almost won an upset in her race for district attorney in Queens, New York. On election night, Caban tweeted, "We have built the most powerful, the most diverse, the most beautiful coalition that a borough-wide race has ever seen. From formerly incarcerated folks to

64 Andrew Barr, Twitter, April 12, 2019, https://twitter.com/RepAndyBarr/status/1116802528459595776.
65 Ron Klain, Twitter, April 17, 2019, https://twitter.com/ronaldklain/status/1118618387494600704?s=11.

sex workers to undocumented immigrants to community-based organizations & activists to local & national elected officials."[66] At the end of July 2019, the race was called for her opponent by a very slim margin after a recount.[67]

Caban, a queer public defender, was an unusual candidate for DA who promised to be a reformer rather than just a "lock-'em-up" prosecutor. Nearly defeating Melinda Katz, the borough president, who was widely expected to win, Caban had put together, with AOC's support, a coalition similar to the one that had sent AOC to Congress. It is clear that AOC, and now Caban, have changed politics for good in that part of New York City. They're here to stay. "We meet a machine with a movement." Ocasio-Cortez tweeted, adding an emoji of a flexed bicep.[68] We have power and we are going to use it. AOC also reflected back on the year that had gone by, tweeting "Today marks one year since I won my primary election. It has been a transformative year for myself, our community, and the overall progressive movement. As I reflect throughout the day, the main sentiment I want to share with you all is: Thank you."[69] No one is going to underestimate her going forward.

---

66 Tiffany Caban, Twitter, June 25, 2019, https://twitter.com/CabanForQueens/status/1143722804468207616?ref.
67 Vivian Wang, "The Queens D.A. Race Has a Winner. Here's Why It's Still Not Over," *New York Times,* July 29, 2019, https://www.nytimes.com/2019/07/29/nyregion/melinda-katz-caban-queens-da.html.
68 Alexandria Ocasio-Cortez, Twitter, June 25, 2019, https://twitter.com/AOC/status/1143720129878011904?ref.
69 Alexandria Ocasio-Cortez, Twitter, June 26, 2019, https://twitter.com/AOC/status/1143905957153558528.

★ ★ ★

I quoted Bobby Riggs and Billie Jean King at the beginning of this chapter, because King is such an icon and her experience shows that, even for strong women like her, it is hard to find respect, even when you prove over and over your talent and drive. Stats don't lie: women suffer from lower pay (only 79 cents on the dollar compared to men), compose less than 20 percent of members of corporate boards, and even now after a record year of women being elected to Congress, make up only 20 percent of that body. Sexual harassment hasn't stopped despite the #MeToo moment and movement. That's why King continues to tell women to fight for respect and higher pay but also to start by valuing themselves. She urges women not to be afraid to make demands. To prepare to make an ask, women should practice by imagining the process, including preparing for a negative answer. "If there's a 'no,' there's another opportunity some other place," said King. "Keep going. Ask for what you want and need. Do your homework. Most CEOs are men, so we have to convince them to give us what we want."

Bustle is right to say that "King may have won the Battle of the Sexes in 1973, but it's clear that there are still many battles yet to be won on behalf of women everywhere—on and off the court." It wasn't really about tennis; it was about self-respect and fighting for the respect of others. It was about forcing others, especially men, to take women seriously. Tennis was just the forum for the fight. The rest of us have these daily skirmishes in the office, at home, at school, and some, like AOC, in the halls of Congress.[70] The daily toll can be great as we constantly face petty criticism and derision. But don't let them underestimate you—and don't underestimate yourself. Words to live by.

How can we make sure that the slow drip of underestimation doesn't erode our self-esteem in the long term? Can we hope that the regular and consistent pushback and examples of women like AOC and Billie Jean King will end the tyranny of condescension? I think so. And I have to hope so; in the arc of history, the more women are visible and the more they fight, the more the world changes for the better. Senator Elizabeth Warren provides a useful example of why staying in the fight matters. Senate Majority Leader Mitch McConnell tried to silence her when she was reading a letter from Coretta Scott King in her fight against the confirmation of attorney general nominee Sen. Jeff Sessions. Using his prerogatives as the Senate's leader, McConnell relied on an obscure Senate rule to shut her down. As he did so, he said, "Senator Warren was giving a lengthy speech. She had appeared to violate the rule. She was warned. She was given an explanation. Nevertheless, she persisted."

---

70   Anna Klassen, "The Real Reason Billie Jean King Beat Bobby Riggs Has Nothing to do with Tennis," *Bustle,* September 22, 2017, https://www.bustle.com/p/the-real-reason-billie-jean-king-beat-bobby-riggs-has-nothing-to-do-with-tennis-2375744.

And "she persisted" became our mantra. Because Warren did, and does, and so does AOC. So must we all.

That is, we need to persist because we all know that even after regularly hitting balls out of the park, women continue to be underestimated and disregarded. Despite all of her success as a new member of Congress, AOC still faces a barrage of criticism and taunts for not being smart. But with patience and even good humor, she destroys her opponents with the back of her hand. When she sent her followers the message on Twitter that "you can't wait for hope. You have to be hope," Kurt Schlichter tweeted back, "I hope you'll spew better cliches." Never to waste an opportunity for education, Ocasio-Cortez replied on Twitter, "What, are you sad I don't speak as our President does, w top hits like 'Just grab 'em by the p—?' Or going on abt turbines & wind cancer? I could win a Nobel Prize in Physics & they'd still call me dumb. That's why I don't give a damn about misogynist takes on my intelligence."[71] Score: AOC 1, opponent 0.

---

71 Alexandria Ocasio-Cortez, Twitter, May 29, 2019, https://twitter.com/aoc/status/1133892883264823302?s=11

CHAPTER THREE

Your Life Is Your Life

[AOC's] commitment to putting power in the hands of the people is forged in fire. Coming from a family in crisis and graduating from school with a mountain of debt, she fought back against a rigged system and emerged as a fearless leader . . . She reminds all of us that even while greed and corruption slow our progress, even while armies of lobbyists swarm Washington, in our democracy, true power still rests with the people. And she's just getting started.

—Senator Elizabeth Warren, writing in *Time*'s annual roundup of the 100 most influential people.[72]

To which Alexandria Ocasio-Cortez gracefully replied via Twitter, "Couldn't be more honored and humbled to read these words from a woman I admire so deeply. Thank you, Senator Warren, for your tireless

---

72　Elizabeth Warren, "Alexandria Ocasio-Cortez," *Time,* 2019, http://time.com/collection/100-most-influential-people-2019/5567752/alexandria-ocasio-cortez/.

fight for working families."[73] Let's pause for a minute to consider what it means for such a young person to make this list—someone who has been on the national stage for such a short time. It really underscores how she has delivered a shock to the system, a shock it needed. She didn't make it by selling out her ideals but by living them and by relying on her own life experiences to relate to average people and the struggles they face.

It was those challenging experiences that propelled the young activist into the race for elected office. She was born in Parkchester, a part of the Bronx, in 1989. Her dad was originally from the South Bronx, from a Puerto Rican family, and owned a small business. He was an architect and had a small company doing building design. Her mother was born in Puerto Rico and still had a large family on the island. According to her campaign flyers, the family was working-class and her mother worked as a housecleaner. Everyone took part in making ends meet.[74] While in high school, Alexandria often pitched in to help her mother in her housecleaning job at neighbors' houses and even applied to college using an essay describing how she and her mother had shared duties helping a recently widowed man by cleaning his kitchen.[75] Even though the trolls of the right attacked her because she "really" went to

73   Alexandria Ocasio-Cortez, Twitter, April 17, 2019, https://twitter .com/aoc/status/1118528576209526785?s=11

74   "Meet Alexandria," AOC Campaign Website, accessed August 16, 2019, https://web.archive.org/web/20180627143050/https://www .ocasio2018.com/about.

75   Charlotte Alter, "'Change Is Closer Than We Think.' Inside Alexandria Ocasio-Cortez's Unlikely Rise," *Time*, March 21, 2019, http://time.com/longform/alexandria-ocasio-cortez-profile/.

school in Yorktown, AOC never contended she had spent her entire life in the Bronx.[76] Instead her campaign materials explained that even as a child, she understood how slanted the playing was in favor of the wealthy, including how much better are the schools for the children of the privileged. Her parents determined that she should go to school in Yorktown rather than the Bronx, ensuring that "much of her life was defined by the 40 minute commute between school and her family in the Bronx. It was clear to her, even then, that the zip code a child was born in determined much of their destiny. The 40 minute drive represented a vastly different quality of available schooling, economic opportunity, and health outcomes."[77]

Being able to live in Yorktown and attend its better schools took the help of her whole family.[78] "My entire extended family—my tias, my grandparents, everybody—all chipped in so we could get a down payment on a tiny home 40 minutes north of the Bronx, in a school

76 Mathew Iglesias, "Conservatives' Obsession with Alexandria Ocasio-Cortez's High School, Explained," *Vox*, January 4, 2019, https://www.vox.com/2019/1/4/18167175/alexandria-ocasio-cortez-sandy-yorktown-high-school.

77 "Meet Alexandria," AOC Campaign Website, accessed August 16, 2019, https://web.archive.org/web/20180627143050/https://www.ocasio2018.com/about.

78 Alexandra Ma and Eliza Relman, "Meet Alexandria Ocasio-Cortez, the millennial, socialist political novice who's now the youngest woman ever elected to Congress," *Business Insider*, January 8, 2019, https://www.businessinsider.com/all-about-alexandria-ocasio-cortez-who-beat-crowley-in-ny-dem-primary-2018-6#her-parents-were-disappointed-in-their-local-schooling-system-so-her-extended-family-helped-fund-a-move-to-a-better-school-district-2.

district that was a little bit better than the one I was born into," she said to *The Intercept*. "It was a reality of my life. That 40-minute drive, from where I went to school to where my family spent their time, kind of told the whole story."[79] The transition to schooling in Yorktown wasn't always easy, as AOC faced cultural barriers to her success as a Puerto Rican. Certain fashions for women in the Bronx, like big hoop earrings or necklaces sporting one's name, were not seen as "appropriate." Called "Sandy" when younger, Alexandria learned how to operate in both settings, understanding the coded language of class and race in America.[80]

But that forty-minute drive became the symbol for her right-wing attackers of her lack of authenticity, evidence that she had "made up" her ethnic roots and working-class background. They clearly missed the obvious. Her story resonated because it was so similar to that of many other families who struggle to get their kids a better education and a better chance than they have had. As *Vox* reporter Matt Yglesias put it, "In fact, it's likely that no previous congressional candidate's high school career has ever been subjected to as much scrutiny as Ocasio-Cortez." But what also confused her critics was

79   Aida Chavez and Ryan Grim, "A Primary Against the Machine: A Bronx Activist Looks to Dethrone Joseph Crowley, the King of Queens," *The Intercept*, May 22, 2018 https://theintercept.com/2018/05/22/joseph-crowley-alexandra-ocasio-cortez-new-york-primary/.

80   Charlotte Alter, "'Change Is Closer Than We Think.' Inside Alexandria Ocasio-Cortez's Unlikely Rise," *Time*, March 21, 2019, http://time.com/longform/alexandria-ocasio-cortez-profile/.

her success at school and obvious intellect. The focus on AOC's high school years, Yglesias noted, was "in part simply because she's very young and was in high school very recently. But she was also a noteworthy high school student who won a prestigious ISEF science fair prize in 2007 and consequently had an asteroid named after her."[81] The Right could not fathom this fact—AOC is a smart young Latinx politician and has come from a financially strapped background that has had a major impact on her policies and politics.

Every day, AOC connects her work to her life experience. She is a model for how challenging circumstances can inform and shape one's life's work. Indeed, you might say such experiences must shape our work in order for us to be effective. Her authenticity allows her to be a big, bold voice for her values. When her father's death from cancer plunged the family into economic instability, she took two jobs to help her mother try to hold on to the family home, which was in foreclosure. Waiting tables and bartending to add to her mother's income as a house cleaner and school-bus driver, AOC has directly experienced life on the brink of financial collapse. And with Hurricane Maria in Puerto Rico, she lost a nursing home–bound grandfather who died in the hurricane's aftermath. The struggles her family faced are common,

---

81 Mathew Iglesias, "Conservatives' Obsession with Alexandria Ocasio-Cortez's High School, Explained," *Vox*, January 4, 2019, https://www.vox.com/2019/1/4/18167175/alexandria-ocasio-cortez-sandy-yorktown-high-school.

but there are few lifelines for those facing poverty and bankruptcy.

In college, she was already a leader. Speaking to the assembled students at Boston University on Martin Luther King Day in 2011, she was asked by the dean to respond to the question, derived from King's teachings, "Can this be the generation that's great, Sandy?" "Let's see," Ocasio-Cortez said. Very polished already as a speaker, she also had a well-honed message for her audience. "Greatness has never been a result of circumstance or fortune," she said. "It is not an inherited trait or a function of destiny. Greatness is reserved for the delinquents, the combatants of the status quo."[82] She was precocious on the stage, showing a comfort with public speaking that usually comes only with age and experience—and for some, never arrives. As an example that would make many students of foreign languages envious, she was even able to give a talk to the assembled faculty in French at the end of her semester abroad junior year, which she spent in Niger. She hadn't known any French at the beginning of the semester.

Besides her talent for public speaking and language, AOC also excelled in science. In high school, she placed

---

82 Eliza Relman, "The Truth About Alexandria Ocasio-Cortez," *Insider,* January 6, 2019, https://www.insider.com/alexandria-ocasio-cortez-biography-2019-1.

second in microbiology in a contest held by the Intel International Science and Engineering Fair. Her project: a study of roundworms and the impact of antioxidants on their longevity. Calling herself "dorky,"[83] Ocasio-Cortez has helped with the efforts of advocates in STEM—or Science, Technology, Engineering and Math—to make these subjects accessible to girls and women, who are often trolled or discouraged from participating. It's worth noting how valuable it is to have a young, prominent, and successful woman embrace her smart side.

At Boston University (BU), she was a leader in many ways, including being a convener on Friday afternoons for something called Coffee and Conversations. After wide-ranging debates on a variety of topics that would last for a couple of hours, she would bring the discussion to a close with her personal take. And she didn't hesitate to take the conversation in challenging directions. "It was always a little bit edgy—she wasn't afraid to take us to the next level," said Bruna Maia, a BU classmate. In addition to the discussion group, AOC was also in charge of BU's Alianza Latina and met with Boston-area students on issues around the economy and student loans. She thought this was all completely normal for a college student. "I didn't understand why people called me an activist," she told *Insider*. "I felt like I was just saying things that were very common sense. I would just say,

---

83   Charlotte Alter, "'Change Is Closer Than We Think.' Inside Alexandria Ocasio-Cortez's Unlikely Rise," *Time*, March 21, 2019, http://time.com/longform/alexandria-ocasio-cortez-profile/.

'Hey, kids in the Bronx should have a good education.' And they'd be, like, 'Oh, she's an activist.' And I was, like, why is it when I say these things I'm an activist, but when this person says these things they're just a responsible parent or auntie or whatever?"

Some of her friends simply derived hope from her leadership and action agenda. Her friend Maia said, "We would say 'Sandy for president' because we were, like, 'Yes, you're speaking my truth right now.'"[84]

Maybe it's a cliché, but it's inescapable that you come from somewhere, and that past and that place shapes who you are. As in AOC's case, that place is one of financial straits and high expectations. A family that sacrificed a lot to give her more than they could really afford. A young adulthood with a terrible loss and further economic struggles. But also a close-knit family that gave her much support, including the willingness of her relatives to pitch in to help her attend better schools than she could have gone to in the Bronx as well as parents whose love enabled her to value herself and gain the confidence so many of us lack. While not all of us have had that kind of support and affection in our lives, we are still the products of our upbringings. Sometimes that means learning from the heartache. If we can understand

---

84 Eliza Relman, "The Truth About Alexandria Ocasio-Cortez," *Insider*, January 6, 2019, https://www.insider.com/alexandria-ocasio-cortez-biography-2019-1.

why and how our own circumstances were challenging, perhaps we can help others avoid that pain. Or perhaps it can shape our decisions whether to pursue careers or projects encouraged by our families and communities, or whether we should escape their negative influence.

For some, the first step is analysis. That can be either the formal kind, if it's necessary or desired, with a doctor or therapist or teacher or mentor, or the informal kind that involves keeping a journal, looking inward, and asking questions about oneself. But for all of us, it is important not to overdo the self-criticism or blaming. Even if there's blame to go around, spending a lot of time in recrimination isn't healthy. If we can put down the burden of holding on to blame (not easy and not possible for all people, I know), we can carry a lighter load along our path. AOC is a lucky one who seems to have had a happy childhood and, despite money challenges, she had access to a good education and grew up safe, secure, and loved. But she did not forget those financial struggles and the toll they took on her family. For her, her father's untimely death and the resulting precarious economic position pitched her family into a difficult time. They pulled through, but that experience and her work as a wage laborer and organizer helped shape her decisions about her future career—she wanted to help people avoid the precarity her family had faced. That's not always easy for people—to use their personal experiences, both positive and negative, to better understand how others' lives are similarly affected and to use that knowledge to set life goals.

When she ran for Congress, she already had a vision of social justice, having worked as a political organizer on Bernie Sanders's 2016 presidential campaign and in Senator Ted Kennedy's office as an intern working on immigration cases while in college. In 2008, during the worst part of the great recession, her family was hit with another crisis. In an interview with *The Intercept*, AOC described the night she found out her father was dying. Only nineteen years old and in college at Boston University, Ocasio-Cortez got a call from her mother while in class, asking her to come home immediately. She had last seen her dad just before leaving for college that fall. "I didn't know that it was going to be the last time that I talked to my dad, but toward the end of our interaction, I started to feel like it was," Ocasio-Cortez recalled. "I said goodbye, but I think he knew, and I knew. And so I started to leave, and he kind of hollered out, and I turned around in the doorframe, and he said, 'Hey, make me proud.'"[85]

That's why when her mother called that day, AOC feared the worst. Running out of the lecture hall, she grabbed a cab to the airport and flew back to New York City on the next available flight. Her father was in the hospital already, so she went directly there to see him. He died soon after. Only able to take a week off from classes, she had to return to Boston without adequate

85 Charlotte Alter, "'Change Is Closer Than We Think.' Inside Alexandria Ocasio-Cortez's Unlikely Rise," *Time*, March 21, 2019, http://time.com/longform/alexandria-ocasio-cortez-profile/.

time for her family or for her sorrow. "I come from a working-class background, so you don't really get a ton of time to mourn," she said. College was too valuable and too expensive to lose precious days even if her psyche needed them desperately. And there's no doubt that her dad's last words to her—"make me proud"—left their mark.

Finances, already precarious, only got worse for the family after her father's death. In addition to the student loan debt AOC had taken on to get to college, the Great Recession took its toll on the family's bank account. On top of that, the family was involved in a long legal dispute with the Westchester County Surrogate's Court because her father had died without leaving a will. According to Alexandria Ocasio-Cortez, the court-appointed lawyers took advantage of the family to earn fees at their expense, as they sunk "deeper and deeper underwater," she said.[86] She felt that they had been victims of a predatory bureaucracy that can inflict further harm on vulnerable people who are not versed in the intricacies of the system. Ocasio-Cortez ran up against a well-documented corrupt system that had taken advantage of many poor and naive families. In a *New York Times* article from 2011, which incidentally called Joe Crowley "the party boss in Queens," the newspaper evoked a dystopia of corruption

---

86   Aida Chavez and Ryan Grim, "A Primary Against the Machine: A Bronx Activist Looks to Dethrone Joseph Crowley, the King of Queens," *The Intercept*, May 22, 2018 https://theintercept.com/2018/05/22/joseph-crowley-alexandria-ocasio-cortez-new-york-primary/.

and legal complexity, a combination of Tammany Hall and *The Pickwick Papers*:

> Power and money are found not so much in the voting booth as in the machine-controlled judicial conventions that pick judges, and in the court-house on Sutphin Boulevard. That is where you find Surrogate's Court, otherwise known as widows and orphans court. This court appoints guardians who make handsome fees processing the estates of those Queens residents who die without wills. To enter this court is to stumble upon Ponce de Leon's own spring, an eternal source of easy money for the politically wired.[87]

Several of Crowley's attorneys got assigned the work of administering the estates of those who had died without wills, making millions in the process. In fact, one of them, Gerard Sweeney, who served as counsel to the public administrator of the court from 2006 to 2017, took home $30 million.[88]

Her mother's job as a domestic worker cleaning houses and as a bus driver didn't bring in much money

87   Michael Powell, "A Court, Not Votes, Sustains a Political Machine in Queens," *New York Times,* November 29, 2011, https://www .nytimes.com/2011/11/29/nyregion/in-queens-political-center-is-in-surrogates-court.html.

88   Ross Barkan, "Three Lawyers Control the Queens Democratic Party While One Rakes Millions from Surrogate's Court Wills," *New York Daily News,* April 2, 2017, https://www.nydailynews.com/news/politics/ lawyers-controlled-queens-dems-party-30-years-article-1.3017007.

for the family to survive on, especially with her father's estate tied up in probate and whatever little money was left being eaten up by the appointed "guardians." So AOC, after she got her degree from Boston University, came back to New York to help. She began to chip in some financial support by working as a tipped employee, waiting tables and tending bar in restaurants. She also went to work at the National Hispanic Institute, an advocacy group that focuses on leadership development for young Latinx, where she focused on education issues. Like many families who face economic challenges, they struggled to avoid losing their house as the banks circled, eying the precious asset hungrily. "We just couldn't afford to keep our home, and we had bankers going up to the curb of our home and taking photos of our house," said AOC.[89] It took the Ocasio-Cortez family four years to emerge from the financial turmoil that had followed her father's death, and it was only in 2012 that they could kiss the Westchester surrogate court's oversight goodbye, with a welcome sigh of relief. Nonetheless, in 2016, they didn't have the financial wherewithal to keep the house any longer and AOC's mother and grandmother put it on the market to avoid having the banks take it away from them.[90] AOC's mother and grandmother left New York City in search of cheaper living quarters in Florida,

89 Aida Chavez and Ryan Grim, "A Primary Against the Machine: A Bronx Activist Looks to Dethrone Joseph Crowley, the King of Queens," *The Intercept*, May 22, 2018 https://theintercept.com/2018/05/22/joseph-crowley-alexandra-ocasio-cortez-new-york-primary/.
90 Ibid.

leaving her behind in the Bronx. Despite having to give up the house, Ocasio-Cortez knew it could have been worse. At least they were able to avoid foreclosure and make some money on the sale of the house, something that other people on the brink of financial collapse had not managed.

Life was not easy for Ocasio-Cortez back in New York. Her wages were meager, and she had expenses like health-care coverage that cost her $200 per month. She could not afford to get sick because the deductible was so high it would have decimated her finances. And of course, like so many other college students who are not from affluent families, she still had debt from her college loans, around $25,000 worth, which added another $300 to her monthly expenses.[91] Between health care, student debt, rent, and food, there was not much left over. Remembering those difficult—and still quite recent—days, she made clear that her personal experiences helped give her insights into policy issues that desperately need addressing. "We have an entire generation that is delaying or forgoing purchasing houses," she said to Charlotte Alter of *Time*. "Our entire economy is slowing down due to the student-loan crisis."[92]

It was while working for low wages at the restaurant that she began to get serious about running for Congress.

---

91 Charlotte Alter, "'Change Is Closer Than We Think.' Inside Alexandria Ocasio-Cortez's Unlikely Rise," *Time*, March 21, 2019, http://time.com/longform/alexandria-ocasio-cortez-profile/.
92 Ibid.

A regular, Scott Starrett, came frequently to Flats Fix, the taqueria where Ocasio-Cortez tended bar. He was a recent inhabitant of the city, having just moved from Austin, and missed good tacos. AOC was a lively and warm presence in the bar, and Starrett became friendly with her. Many of their conversations revolved around the 2016 presidential election, and AOC engaged with Starrett and his graphic design-firm colleagues in discussions about politics. "Everyone just loved Sandy," Starrett said to *Business Insider*. "She had an infectious kindness, an infectious presence." "Sandy" talked to him about her experience interning in Senator Kennedy's office while at BU, and he shared his experience working on Texas political campaigns. She began to help out as a volunteer for Bernie Sanders.

After Trump's election, AOC decided to travel to North Dakota to take part in a mobilization, organized by Native Americans, against the Dakota Access Oil pipeline—and she visited Flint, Michigan, along the way in solidarity with the families who had suffered from lead contamination in their water. She brought along a camera that Starrett had loaned to her so she could take pictures of the demonstration. When she came back, she had started to consider throwing her hat in the ring to win the congressional seat in the Bronx. Her younger brother, Gabriel, had made sure her name was known to the group Brand New Congress, which had grown out of Bernie Sanders's campaign and was focused on getting new and diverse progressive candidates to run for Congress. Brand

New Congress saw her potential and gave her a call right away to see if she would run in the 14th District, located in the Bronx and Queens. "We looked at the brother telling the story of a sister who wasn't a giant nonprofit executive, she didn't go work on the Hill for 10 years," Alexandra Rojas recalled. Rojas, who now serves as executive director of Justice Democrats, saw how AOC could relate to her constituents. Her personal experiences gave her candidacy strength in their eyes. As Rojas said, "she was someone who watched her family struggle through the financial crisis."[93] It took some work persuading her to run, but a couple of months after coming back from North Dakota, she was officially a candidate for public office.

Her campaign was made up of people who had founded the Justice Democrats and Brand New Congress, who came to New York to get the inspiring future congresswoman into office, camping out on couches in friends' apartments to keep expenses down. They didn't have a lot of campaign experience or a traditional approach to running an operation, but somehow it worked. These campaign operatives helped the new candidate think through her policies and polish her media presence. And she gathered a group of volunteers to canvass the district. She soon quit her job at the taco bar. Her fan base from the restaurant, Starrett and his colleagues, used their expertise in graphic design to help her with campaign materials. One notable effort included a poster that was

---

93   Ibid.

based on an original from an organizing campaign of the United Farm Workers of America. *Business Insider* commented that "It could've been mistaken for a Netflix show ad. In blaring-blue and yellow block type alongside an image of Sandy, it read 'Ocasio!'"[94] And with the help of a couple young filmmakers, AOC developed a video that quickly went viral focused on economic inequality. Its compelling message and AOC's charismatic voice helped drive more fundraising and media attention and brought a flood of volunteers to the campaign. It also impressed someone who was engaged in the same project as AOC. Ayanna Pressley too was a young woman of color challenging an incumbent white man who had the support of the Democratic insiders. She told *Insider* about playing and replaying the video, and proclaiming "Hell yes." "I was struck by her rawness, her conviction—she'll hate me saying this—her beauty," said Pressley, now Massachusetts' first black congresswoman.[95] Part of that "beauty," was the honesty and authenticity of the candidate in telling her story.

Ocasio-Cortez also benefited from the actors who joined to help out as volunteers. Jake DeGroot, an activist and former theater lighting designer, hosted her first event. Impressed by her intelligence and charisma, he signed on as a volunteer and then became her digital

---

94   Eliza Relman, "The Truth About Alexandria Ocasio-Cortez," *Insider,* January 6, 2019, https://www.insider.com/alexandria-ocasio-cortez-biography-2019-1.
95   Ibid.

organizing director. He was joined by many others from the theater profession, actors and others who brought a surfeit of creative ideas to the nascent campaign. "Theater and politics are very simpatico," explained DeGroot. "Theater done well is politics; politics done poorly is theater."[96]

It was with social media that AOC really powered her campaign. Ocasio-Cortez recognized the advantage of being able to speak in a personal way, but to millions of viewers. It also meant that she could bypass the media that referred to her only as "Crowley's opponent." That's no way to get name recognition. She wasn't born a social media adept, but she was a natural. At the start of her campaign, in May 2017, she was a normal person on Twitter, registering under three hundred followers, and had a handful of likes and other measures of support on some other platforms. In short order, however, she grew her fanbase on Twitter and got to over sixty thousand by the time primary day rolled around. "It was literally just through tweeting and getting that feedback and learning through commentary and testing messages," she said. "Because every time you tweet something how it performs is basically like an A/B test." And since winning the primary, AOC has surpassed the two-million mark on Twitter, which puts her in a special class of social media stars and well beyond where other members

96   Charlotte Alter, "'Change Is Closer than We Think.' Inside Alexandria Ocasio-Cortez's Unlikely Rise," *Time*, March 21, 2019, http://time.com/longform/alexandria-ocasio-cortez-profile/.

of Congress are. She has a breezy and approachable tone, letting people into her life. It's not so different from how she tended bar, open and friendly and making customers feel like they are friends and not just the source of tips. She ranges from political issues and policy debates to discussions about cooking and even her amazed discovery of a garbage disposal in her Washington, DC, apartment. Like many New Yorkers, she had never been exposed to the noisy and sort of creepy appliance and showed that on her Instagram feed. It's that combination of the personal and political that makes her feed especially appealing. Unlike many politicians, she doesn't filter out her own experiences but relates them to the policy ideas she is promoting—and she isn't afraid of showing that she's not an expert at everything (i.e., she had no idea what a garbage disposal was).

"She's willing to let people see her fears, and she's willing to let people see her hesitancies, and she's willing to let people see a process that normally is shadowed," her campaign manager said. And her tweets and posts are not curated or ghostwritten.[97] She also doesn't hesitate to call out or spank her ideological foes, and when she does, it is both funny and informative. Her feed is fresh because it is not one note—it's personal and political, policy and polemics, cooking and kvetching.

Many of us are hesitant to show that much of

---

97 Eliza Relman, "The Truth About Alexandria Ocasio-Cortez," *Insider,* January 6, 2019, https://www.insider.com/alexandria-ocasio-cortez-biography-2019-1.

ourselves. It feels dangerous to expose our private side, especially our fears and anxieties. But there's a benefit to learning how to channel our life experience in a positive way to improve our work and personal interactions. For one, it can give us empathy, which allows us to understand and address the challenges others face. By looking at our own experiences as knowledge gained rather than as something to be ashamed of or hide, we can learn how to forgive or at least tolerate better the idiosyncrasies and personality tics of our friends and colleagues. It also allows us to think through broader questions of how to structure society—was our experience typical or an anomaly? Could it be improved through policy changes or revised practices? That means we can think about the world as an informed citizen, not just based on what we read in the paper or on the Internet but what we read in our own lives. While despair is rarely a positive emotion in our lives, anger can be, so long as it is channeled. A righteous anger directed at making the world better can also provide solace for our own personal emotional turmoil.

Having seen how a health care crisis can pitch a middle-class family into the abyss, AOC has championed Medicare for All, believing that health care is a human right. On her campaign website, Ocasio-Cortez says "Almost every other developed nation in the world has universal health-care. It's time the United States catch up to the rest of the world in ensuring all people have real healthcare coverage that doesn't break the bank." In part because of her forceful advocacy, most of the Democrats who have announced that they are running for president in 2020 have endorsed the idea. Like Elizabeth Warren, who as a law professor analyzed the relationship between a health setback and bankruptcy, AOC sees the direct connection between the ability to live a middle-class life and an accessible, affordable health-care system.

This same approach characterized her willingness to be filmed for a documentary right from the start of her campaign. She believed that it would help other non-traditional candidates understand the process, especially the financial struggles for someone who works a job for tips or minimum wage. Rachel Lears, the film's director, along with Robin Blotnick, her husband, cowriter, and editor, sought to use the stories of Ocasio-Cortez and three other women who were fighting uphill battles for election against Democratic incumbents to illustrate how power can change hands. "I hope that this story does push people to think about participating in different ways," said Lears.[98] That documentary, *Knock Down the House*, was released on Netflix. While mostly focused on Ocasio-Cortez, in part because of the budget constraints facing the New York City–based documentarians, the film showed the toll of campaigning on all the women as well as the ways that their shared struggles brought them together—and informed their candidacies. Amy Vilela,

---

98 Melena Ryzik, "How Alexandria Ocasio-Cortez's Triumph, 'Ugly Crying' and All, Was Captured," *New York Times*, May 3, 2019, https://www.nytimes.com/2019/05/03/movies/knock-down-the-house-netflix.html.

who like AOC was running for the House, had to give up her job in finance and use the sale of her house to fund her campaign. "We had to downsize everything," she said. "We ended up going into debt." She wanted to be part of a political shift "more than I loved the benefits of my lifestyle and the career I held."[99] Vilela, like the other two women profiled besides AOC, lost her race. When Vilela fell short on primary night, Ocasio-Cortez reached out to her via phone to express her sadness. "What I love about the vulnerability that we see, throughout this entire film from everybody—it shows the world a different model of strength," Ocasio-Cortez said. "You know, I'm like ugly crying on a screen."[100] AOC was well aware that her crying would be the subject of trolling and efforts to humiliate her, but she was undaunted. "I already know they're going to screen grab shots of me crying and make memes out of it. I think the fact that you have nothing to hide is a huge and intimidating strength," she said. That's something to think about—showing your vulnerabilities can actually be a sign of strength.

Another candidate, Cori Bush, running in St. Louis, Missouri, was also seeking to shake up the status quo and bring the community's concerns to the forefront. And she sought to make sure her life and experiences on the job and elsewhere were part of her campaign—like AOC, she argued that she could better represent the people of the district than long-term incumbent congressman Lacy

---

99   Ibid.
100   Ibid.

Clay. And she also rejected the warnings that she should hide her true self in order to run. "I heard things, wow," she said, like, "I need to have a husband in order to run. I also heard that I needed to change my hair, that braids looked unprofessional. And if I wanted to get into certain rooms with real people who were real donors, I could never look like a nurse." Bush knew that, like AOC, she needed to speak from her actual experiences, not run from them. "Representation is important," she said. "I'm a nurse because I saw a black woman working as a nurse and that taught me that I can do this. And in the same way, I want other black girls to see that it's O.K., that you can do this." Bush may have lost that race but, determined to win in 2020, she is running again.[101]

Considering three of the four subjects of *Knock Down the House* lost their bids to unseat incumbents, the filmmakers might have decided to pivot and focus only on the young New Yorker. But that wouldn't have done justice to AOC and her efforts because she never saw herself as in the race alone. "Sometimes when I'm in DC, people think I'm like this alien, you know?" she said. And she wants people to know how hard it was for her to get to Washington and the struggles of the others who might have joined her: "Because you see the blood, sweat, and tears that it took just for us to get a seat at the table. It brings a different intensity and urgency." And it has another therapeutic effect for AOC—it also underscores the importance of what she is trying to accomplish in

---

101   Ibid.

DC. "It's a reminder of the energy that it took to get here, and what an enormous opportunity this is. It makes me feel like I have to squeeze every drop out of it."[102]

AOC speaks to younger Americans because she understands the economic struggles so many of them face. While the economy seems to be in decent shape in the aggregate, most of the benefits, actually the vast majority of those benefits, go to older wealthy white men. Younger people and economically vulnerable groups have not shared in the alleged prosperity of twenty-first-century America. She knows how hard it is to live by piecing together short-term and temporary jobs. "Spoiler alert: the gig economy is about not giving people full-time jobs," she stated to *Time*. "So it should be no secret why millennials want to decouple your insurance status from your employment status."[103] For more and more Americans, the new normal is not a job for ten to twenty years but a series of—or the simultaneous holding of—multiple jobs with no benefits and no security. Without access to affordable health care outside of the employment context, this group of workers faces the daily stress of worrying when the next illness might hit them or when their children might get sick or injured. AOC's personal experiences give her direct insight into one of our century's greatest public-policy emergencies.

---

102   Ibid.

103   Charlotte Alter, "'Change Is Closer Than We Think.' Inside Alexandria Ocasio-Cortez's Unlikely Rise," *Time*, March 21, 2019, http://time.com/longform/alexandria-ocasio-cortez-profile/.

Her fight for students who suffer under massive debt is similarly tied to her own life. In introducing a bill with Senator Bernie Sanders to cancel $1.6 billion in student debt, she lamented that it had actually been less of a challenge for her to get elected to Congress despite her age, sex, and ethnic identity than to pay off her loans. "It was literally easier for me to become the youngest woman in American history elected to Congress than it is for me to pay off my student loan debt," she said. "In order for me to get a chance to have healthcare . . . to pay off my student loans, I had to do something that was nearly impossible," Ocasio-Cortez said. "And I don't think that that is the bar through which a person should be able to access education, healthcare, and a bevy of other things that should be considered human rights." It's wrong to have such a high bar for young people's debt obligations when they are not considered old enough or mature enough to engage in other aspects of adult life, she stated at the press conference. "What we tell 17-year-olds all the time is that 'you are not old enough or responsible enough to drink . . . to vote . . . to serve in our military, but you are old enough and responsible enough to take on a quarter million dollars worth of debt,' and that is wrong," Ocasio-Cortez said.[104] At the same time, we tell Americans that education is vital and that getting a good job depends

---

104 Faris Bseiso, "Alexandria Ocasio-Cortez: It was 'Literally Easier' to Become Youngest Woman in Congress than to Pay Off Student Loans," CNN, June 25, 2019, https://www.cnn.com/2019/06/25/politics/ocasio-cortez-student-loans-congress/index.html.

on it—the dissonance is palpable and again creates emotional and financial stress for younger Americans and their families.

Health care and student debt are existential issues for young workers—they aren't getting insurance from their job, and if they get hurt or sick, that illness could wipe out any savings they have—any they have left, that is, after making their monthly installment on their school loans. That's why so many agree with her that socialism is not a dirty word. Many more millennials and younger Americans have in fact embraced democratic socialism as their ideology.

After AOC won the endorsement from the Democratic Socialists of America, it sent many volunteers to her district to help out with the ground game. It was an important effort, along with the work of her many unpaid volunteers who barnstormed the Bronx and Queens to find any vote they could for AOC. They all knew it was an uphill effort, but they succeeded as she ended up winning by around four thousand votes. The victory in her primary gave her wings to go out and help fellow democratic socialists and progressive candidates in their primary and general election battles. She went to Kansas, Missouri, and Michigan on behalf of other challengers. She didn't have a magic touch—just because she showed up did not mean every candidate would pull through. In fact, the Justice Democrats, with whom she was working, had a high loss rate, with only four of seventy-eight endorsed candidates pulling through. But in a system

where incumbents almost always win, that's not necessarily a bad record.[105]

In any case, it has never just been about elections
for Ocasio-Cortez and her cohort. They want to change
hearts and minds. "The point of a message is not to win
an election—it's to change policy, to move things for
people, to lead with your ideals," explained Dr. Abdul
El-Sayed, thirty-four, a losing candidate for governor of
Michigan. "Who cares about winning elections?"[106] Of
course El-Sayed may have indulged in a bit of an over-
statement, but his point is basically true: elections are in
service of ideas, and the ideas are what is most important
for AOC and her allies.

For example, Ocasio-Cortez has become the face of
one of the biggest new ideas of the current moment: con-
necting climate change to economic issues and dubbing
that concept the Green New Deal.

Along with the other young leaders, Ocasio-Cortez is
not willing to concede her future simply because others
have investments today in fossil fuel, and she has joined
the Sunrise Movement, a group made up of young activists fighting to force their elders to address the climate
crisis. As Ocasio-Cortez said at a press conference with
Sunrise, "What's 'too much' for me is the fact that, in
1989, the year that I was born . . . the year that many

1 5 Charlotte Alter, "'Change Is Closer Than We Think.' Inside
Alexandria Ocasio-Cortez's Unlikely Rise," *Time*, March 21, 2019,
http://time.com/longform/alexandria-ocasio-cortez-profile/.
106 Ibid.

of us were born, and in years after and right before, that politicians were first informed by NASA . . . that climate change was going to threaten my life and everyone here's life to come, and they did nothing. That is too much for me," she said to the crowd. "And I will be damned if the same politicians who refused to act then are going to try to come back today and say we need a middle-of-the-road approach to save our lives."[107] The famous Texas politician and left-wing populist Jim Hightower wrote a book called *There's Nothing in the Middle of the Road but Yellow Stripes and Dead Armadillos: A Work of Political Subversion.* That pretty well sums it up. AOC and her generation increasingly see the clock running out for them and their children and have what political activists have dubbed "the urgency of now." It's now, or it is clearly going to be never.

Some of us have had experiences like that—children of the Cold War era were taught to avoid the fallout from a nuclear weapon by going into the school hallway and curling up on the ground with one's head against a locker. That caused many in that generation to fear nuclear war and spawned political organizations to demand arms control and security measures to control those doomsday weapons, as well as cultural memes like *Dr. Strangelove.* Those forces pushed elected leaders to pursue arms control treaties and deterrence policies to

---

107   Zoe Carpenter, "The Political Power of the Green New Deal," *The Nation,* May 17, 2019, https://www.thenation.com/article/sunrise-movement-green-new-deal-democratic-primary-climate-change/.

avoid such an outcome. Now children are taught to fear guns and that the world might be irrevocably damaged by the time they are old enough to have their own children. Is it any surprise that these two issues—gun violence and climate change—are central to their organizing focus and political agenda? It's their lives or perhaps their early deaths that are driving their engagement. It's not surprising at all.

In November 2016, Ocasio-Cortez coasted to victory as a member of the House of Representatives. She came to Washington and immediately started making a difference, but she didn't change how she lived her life on a daily basis. Nor did she forget about the life experiences that had taught her the challenges of unaffordable healthcare and education, low wages, and a damaged environment. Unwilling to step back like a demure freshman member, she continued to speak out. She was not going to be deferential to lobbyist-driven events or special interest–driven legislation. When the Democrats went to Harvard's Kennedy School for new member orientation, she immediately raised concerns about the programming that had been funded by corporations.[108] She and several

---

108   Katherine Hignett, "Alexandria Ocasio-Cortez Blasts 'Bipartisan Congressional Orientation: 'Lobbyists are Here . . . Where's Labor?'" *Newsweek*, December 7, 2018, https://www.newsweek.com/alexandria-ocasio-cortez-lobbyists-congress-harvard-rashida-tlaib-1248959.

other new members organized a rally on issues they said they had been elected to fight for—health care, climate change, gun control, and economic justice. "This is why the Democrats won. This is why we're in the majority. We refuse to put hope and aspiration and values on a shelf," said AOC friend and fellow new House member, Ayanna Pressley, who had also defeated a long-term Democratic incumbent in Massachusetts. "I was not sent to Washington to play nice."[109] And along with their criticism of the subject matter at Harvard, these new members also disagreed with the funding behind the event. "Our 'bipartisan' Congressional orientation is cohosted by a corporate lobbyist group. Other members have quietly expressed to me their concern that this wasn't told to us in advance," Ocasio-Cortez complained in a tweet. "Lobbyists are here. Goldman Sachs is here. Where's labor? Activists? Frontline community leaders?"[110] Health care and gun violence are among the issues that have shaped these women's lives, and they will bring that to Congress, despite any efforts to thwart them.

But it hasn't all been showing her star power in DC or living off of her Twitter fame for AOC. She has not forgotten where she came from. While some of the old guard continue to dismiss her, she has shown up. Joe

---

109 Eliza Relman, "Alexandria Ocasio-Cortez and other new House progressives are tweeting their dissatisfaction with orientation at Harvard," *Business Insider,* December 6, 2018, https://www.businessinsider.com/alexandria-ocasio-cortez-and-house-freshmen-are-protesting-orientation-harvard-2018-12.
110 Ibid.

Crowley's ally Michael Reich, the head of the Queens Democratic Party, continues to call her a fraud and a carpetbagger. "She isn't a Queens person, but she isn't a Bronx person either," said Reich. "She grew up in Westchester. The family owns two homes. She has this thing that, 'My mother scrubbed floors.' Well, her father was an architect. It's unfortunate he passed away early but they had a home in Yorktown Heights and a condo in the Bronx. She has no connection to Queens at all."[111] Reich clearly doesn't care much for the facts. But here's one: AOC spends time in the district. According to her constituents, she is visible in a way her predecessor was not. "I have seen her more in the past six months than I saw Joe Crowley in the past 10 years," a constituent reported.[112] She's still living her life in the Bronx and Queens as she knows she must in order to serve the people of the district. And she will continue to bring that life experience to Congress, because that is what it means to be a "representative."

Transferring life experience, regardless of the vocation, is an important lesson, and we can all take notes from AOC. Though my own background is quite different from AOC's, I too see the applications of this lesson.

I grew up in the suburbs of Chicago, the child of academics. My father taught history at Northwestern with a

---

111 David Freedlander, "How Alexandria Ocasio-Cortez Broke All the Rules of New York Politics," *Politico*, April 8, 2019, https://www.politico.com/magazine/story/2019/04/08/alexandria-ocasio-cortez-new-york-226578.
112 Ibid.

focus on race in American history and particularly the ideological component of race. So I grew up understanding early on that most of what white people accept about "race" is in fact a creation of dominant groups who graft stereotypes onto skin colors and create false narratives of superiority and inferiority. My mother taught French literature, also at Northwestern. She is just as brilliant as my father, but her career got stuck in a rut because of parenting responsibilities that were not equally shared, and also due to the unexpected arrival of children at a time before birth control was as effective as it can be now.

Both of them have shaped my vision of the world and my desire to try to change it for the better. From my father, I learned to challenge bias and recognize implicit bias as a major feature—not a bug—of how white people view the world and our nation's history. From my mother, I learned that family structures too have built-in structural inequities that are reinforced by how our society regulates schools, work, and recreation. I believe one of the goals of a good society should be to enable people to flourish, and that means helping ensure their talents and desires are not constrained by illegitimate barriers based on wealth, connections, race, or gender. I also learned at home that words are not enough—as enlightened as my father believed himself to be, my mother was still the one doing nine-tenths of the work in the household. So I am a big believer that works must accompany words, even if it is just in one's own home. You have to live your politics or they don't mean all that much.

When I left for college, I decided to study Russian. I won't go into the reasons now, but suffice it to say that it was the end of the Cold War and that made Russian seem interesting. But all through school, I kept ending up involved in politics. So perhaps it was inevitable that when I graduated and could have entered the Foreign Service, I turned down that job offer to come to Washington, DC, with no prospects and no salary. Fortunately, one of my college roommates let me stay with her as I searched for a job on Capitol Hill. In order to pay rent, I waited tables and suffered many a #MeToo moment at a time when we didn't really have a vocabulary for that treatment. I was one of the lucky ones, however, and landed a job after several weeks as a temporary employee for a congressman from Illinois. Representative Lane Evans was a wonderful man, a committed liberal populist—a "prairie populist" to be exact—who believed in fair wages for a day's work and equal treatment for all.

But I was hired away to work on a presidential campaign and went to Iowa, where I was exposed to electoral politics and also to the different groups and individuals who have power in that system. Of particular importance for my future was my connection with labor leaders and union members who formed much of the backbone of Iowa's progressive base—teachers, meatpacking plant and auto parts factory workers, and elected leaders of locals in the district I was working. I deeply connected with the idea that work is a forum for social justice—I knew that as a woman who had been sexually harassed, as someone who believed in racial justice and recognized that our workplaces fall short and that wages are deeply unequal, and as someone who thinks work needs to be fairly rewarded and that all profits should not flow into the pockets of the shareholders and CEOs. Some might think it is funny that I went to Iowa and became a member of the labor movement, but you have to remember that Iowa used to have more of an industrial and populist past.

I didn't love my experience in Iowa as a political organizer, but I did love what I learned—and those lessons have changed the rest of my life.

AOC has taken her life lessons and put them to use in the fight for social justice. Rather than dwell on her family's loss and financial distress, she sought to understand the root causes of that distress and address them through big ideas and political activism. She can provide all of us with a model for how to live our own lives—not to sublimate our personal experiences but to excavate them, examine them, and use them to change the world. Michelle Obama recognized the importance of using one's life as a source of ideas and strength, saying "you should never view your challenges as a disadvantage. Instead, it's important for you to understand that your experience facing and overcoming adversity is actually one of your biggest advantages."[113] Each of us learns

---

113 "Remarks by First Lady at City College of New York Commencement," President Barack Obama White House Archives, June 3, 2016, https://obamawhitehouse.archives.gov/the-press-office/2016/06/03/remarks-first-lady-city-college-new-york-commencement.

important life lessons first as children, in our homes and schools, including when we experience failures and set-backs. It is our ability to learn and grow from those challenges, process the bad, appreciate the good, that makes us stronger and more resilient people. And it makes us human if we can also use our self-awareness to help change the world for others.

CHAPTER FOUR

Don't Accept the Status Quo

WOMEN WHO DISOBEY GENDER NORMS attract trolls and harassers like bees to honey. Not surprisingly, Alexandria Ocasio-Cortez has been swarmed by this particular type of pernicious insect trying to sting her with its "wit" and venom. But she has an uncanny ability to illuminate an issue with a deft tweet or meme—nowhere better than in illustrating the inanity of her misogynistic Internet stalkers. Take for example the insulting tweet of Josh Jordan, who calls himself NumbersMuncher on Twitter. As has happened so frequently, Jordan dismissed Ocasio-Cortez as a fleeting phenomenon with little impact on politics. He tried to use polling results to demonstrate that AOC was unpopular but only referred to her standing with older white men. Clearly, his math skills are poor, as he failed to see that AOC was actually strongly supported by other groups of Americans. Ocasio-Cortez skewered him, tweeting "If you want to know what subconscious bias looks like, it's a headline saying 'AOC is underwater with every group EXCEPT women, nonwhites, and 18-34 year olds,'" she wrote. "So older, conservative white men are considered 'everyone' and everyone else is discounted as an exception." NumbersMuncher later deleted his tweet.[114]

Women are constantly harassed by those who want them to abide by certain acceptable gender norms: "don't be pushy," "don't be demanding," "don't tell people what you want," "don't stand out," and "don't stand up." In other words, don't be a bitch. But women are also told "don't be too smart," "don't be too tall or too short, too fat or too thin, too this or too that." If you don't get treated like an equal, though, it's your fault for not "leaning in." There's always someone who thinks it is his right—or hers sometimes—to comment on our hair, face, or how we walk, talk, or chew gum. It's hard to resist the nonstop pressure to conform to some stereotype of acceptable womanhood. Many young women are policed for being too sporty or "unfeminine." Sometimes from family, even from women family members like grandmothers or sisters, we hear directives like "comb your hair," "it's time to stop doing sports," "why can't you be more like your cousin? She acts in a more feminine way."

114   Alexandria Ocasio-Cortez, Twitter, March 16, 2019, https://twitter
.com/aoc/status/1106953015804731393?s=11.

From men on the street, "smile more," from parents in the neighborhood, "little girls shouldn't get dirty." Girls quickly learn that they are not behaving in a way that society approves of, but they want to climb trees, play baseball, and wear cutoff jeans and their brothers' hand-me-down Little League T-shirts. They might not want to wear frilly dresses, to sit inside on a beautiful day, or to have their snarled hair tugged on by a grandmother—or they might want those things, but not all the time. The constant commentary and criticism ultimately has an impact on how girls and then women behave. Most likely they conform some but hopefully remain a rebel in other ways. But sometimes even that little bit of rebel is hard to keep going. Little girls should not have to give up a part of themselves to "fit in."

But how do we make sure the gender police do not strip girls and women of their individuality through the sniping and whispers, through the shaming and shaping and bullying that we experience from the time we are sentient beings? It is a hard question, but role models like Alexandria Ocasio-Cortez can help give an alternative example for how to behave. AOC has shown that young women can defy the status quo and still be successful—in fact, in her case, her success has been to a great extent a result of her fight to be true to herself. From her first day in Congress, AOC has not allowed conventional wisdom to dissuade her from her goals. Just as she refused to defer to Joe Crowley in the congressional race, she arrived in Congress ready to fight for change, even if that ruffled feathers. For example, during the first day of congressional orientation, she took part in a climate change protest right in front of Nancy Pelosi's office and, while she ultimately supported Pelosi's bid to be speaker, her activism helped extract key concessions and strategic assignments for her and her cohort of newly elected progressive women of color.

Rather than satisfying herself with the micro-legislation of a freshman legislator, Ocasio-Cortez has already begun to work on big ideas, such as Medicare for All, tuition-free public college and trade school, a federal job guarantee, paid family leave, abolishing ICE, ending the privatization of prisons, and enacting gun-control policies. She is probably best known for having pushed the Green New Deal. Here too she challenged the Democrats to move out of their comfort zone, demanding they articulate bold new ideas in the face of a worldwide crisis. The idea of a comprehensive plan to deal with climate change and with economic dislocation, with her backing, has taken off, ultimately pushing several Democratic senators, including Elizabeth Warren, Bernie Sanders, and Cory Booker to support it.

A member of the Democratic Socialists of America, AOC does not shy away from stating her leftist views. On NBC's *Meet the Press*, she related that democratic socialism is "part of what I am. It's not all of what I am. And I think that that's a very important distinction." She does not believe capitalism is the only model, seeing something more egalitarian in the future. That's not a stance very many elected officials are willing to take—that our nation would be better off if capitalism was checked by social justice rules. Elsewhere that would not be an outrageous position. In Sweden, for example, the democratic system has a socialist overlay, ensuring that the fruits of the economy are shared more equitably than in the United States, that women are treated more equally, and that collective concerns, like the rapidly changing climate, are the focus of collective action. Why should that be a radical stance? AOC doesn't think it is.

She has pointed out that some of the most successful government programs would be called socialist by these same critics. The Veterans Health Administration (VHA), for example, provides high-quality health care to millions of veterans for a relatively low cost. Nonetheless, the Trump administration and others on the right are pushing for it to be privatized. Not so fast, say AOC and allies who are fighting legislation to move the VHA from a public system to one run by corporate interests. Ocasio-Cortez points out that the VHA "provides some of the highest quality care to our veterans," blasting efforts by those who would profit from letting "pharmaceutical companies . . . insurance companies, and ultimately . . . a for-profit healthcare industry that does not put people or veterans first" have control over the VHA budget.[115]

---

115 Suzanne Gordon, "AOC Defends an American Socialist Success: Veterans' Health Care," *American Prospect*, April 30 2019, https://prospect.org/article/aoc-defends-american-socialist-success-veterans-health-care.

Not surprisingly, she was quickly vilified by Republicans including a congressman from Tennessee, Phil Roe, who is the highest-ranking Republican on the House Committee on Veterans' Affairs. On Fox News, Congressman Roe said, "Apparently ignorance is bliss when it comes to Representative Ocasio-Cortez and her views of VA," he said. "It is evident that she paid little attention to the scandalous treatment of veterans that occurred several years ago by some in the very agency created to serve them. . . . When you don't know anything about anything you should probably keep your mouth shut or everyone will know you don't know anything."

Yet, as AOC argued, while veterans' care hasn't been perfect by any stretch, it is still better than what the rest of us get. There is a vast body of research detailing the cost efficiencies and superior quality that prevails for veterans over the private-sector health results. At the town hall where AOC spoke, put on by the National Nurses United and the National Nurses Organizing Committee, she was accompanied by the head of Vietnam Veterans of America, John Rowan, who described the shortcomings in terms of the care veterans receive when they cannot access care through the VA health system. In part, the specific types of injuries and health challenges suffered by veterans require specialists, like the doctors in the VA system who are familiar with veterans' health needs. AOC described the multiple and layered concerns of veterans and their families and connected those challenges to the broader effort to reform health care—as well as to the student loan issue she has championed. One reason veterans' health care has suffered, she explained, is because skyrocketing tuition at medical schools and the resulting high debt loads are keeping idealistic young doctors and nurses from pursuing a career in public health.

By making clear to this audience and others that the public approach can be good and indeed even better than a private-sector system, she has undermined the efforts to paint public-sector programs as an unmitigated evil, as "socialism." She compares those who are suffering from a dysfunctional private health-care system to the positive results from the VA and brings both veterans and people who are not in the military together with the understanding that everyone is entitled to a better VA, or certainly to health care that is decent and affordable. She communicates to veterans that the impetus for privatization is not better health care for them but higher profits for providers and more money for spending on hardware that bloats the military-industrial complex. "Care for our veterans should not be for sale," Ocasio-Cortez proclaimed.[116]

People might not think Ocasio-Cortez has much appeal outside of New York, or at least outside of urban areas. But those people are wrong. In fact, it is her proud embrace of her democratic socialism, in defiance of accepted political wisdom, that has made her a star in the most unexpected places. Once she prevailed in her primary bid over Crowley, AOC was much in demand to campaign for other Democratic challengers in states

---

116   Ibid.

as different from New York as Kansas. That's the state where Democratic candidate James Thompson asked the "progressive rocket ship" to stump for him in his uphill battle to win a seat as a democratic socialist.[117] This was AOC's first stop on a whistle-stop tour to support the election of like-minded young idealists. And quite a first stop it was—right into the belly of the beast. The district Thompson hoped to win is the home base of the Koch brothers, the infamous plutocrats who fund conservative causes and who made their money in the oil business. As Sarah Smarsh, a reporter for *The Guardian,* wrote admiringly, "It's one thing to push the Democratic party left in New York City. It is quite another to rabble-rouse for universal healthcare, wind energy and a livable wage in Charles Koch's backyard. Doing so takes, my friends in the northeast might say, 'chutzpah.' Or, as my Kansas farmer grandpa might have said: 'That Jim is full of piss and vinegar.'"[118] Unfortunately neither chutzpah nor the combination of piss and vinegar was enough for Thompson to pull off a win in this district,[119] but his efforts were an admirable fight to bring some sunshine to the swamp of politics as practiced by the billionaire brothers.[120]

---

117   Sarah Smarsh, "They Thought this was Trump Country, Hell No," *The Guardian,* July 26, 2018, https://www.theguardian.com/us-news/2018/jul/26/alexandria-ocasio-cortez-bernie-sanders-kansas-james-thompson.
118   *Id.*
119   Ballotpedia: James Thompson, accessed August 16, 2019, https://ballotpedia.org/James_Thompson_(Kansas).
120   Editor's Note: David Koch passed away during the production of this book, in August 2019.

Thompson appealed to AOC mostly because of his politics but also because of his iconoclasm and stereotype-defying résumé. He was a veteran who practiced civil rights law, representing detained immigrants and people who had suffered brutality at the hands of law enforcement. He also could speak the language of the farmers and working people who made up the district. A believer in women's reproductive rights but also a gun owner, Thompson could break bread—or down a beer—with folks across the spectrum in his district.[121] While his folksiness and feistiness did not carry him across the finish line, he did set a tone of authenticity that marks the new crop of candidates championed by Ocasio-Cortez.

"I had to fight all the time. Literally and figuratively," Thompson said at the rally he held with AOC and Bernie Sanders in July 2018. "That's just part of growing up in poverty. When I see people struggling and I talk about it, I'm not talking about it from up on a hill somewhere." AOC could empathize, having experienced her own set of challenges and come through tested by the fire of critique and underestimation, keeping true to her values and showing those who dismissed her how wrong they were to do so. Reporter Sarah Smarsh, who attended the rally, admired how AOC had "taunted on the Late Show with Stephen Colbert that the current president doesn't know 'how to

121   Sarah Smarsh, "They Thought this was Trump Country, Hell No," *The Guardian*, July 26, 2018, https://www.theguardian.com/us-news/2018/jul/26/alexandria-ocasio-cortez-bernie-sanders-kansas-james-thompson.

deal with a girl from the Bronx.'" Much like the strong and principled Congresswoman Maxine Waters from California who has been targeted with hate messages and death threats for her critiques of the Trump administration, AOC was telling the president he had "'better shoot straight.' This scrappy attitude" wrote Smarsh, "is not the empty bluster of a fearful ego with an orange combover seeking to preserve itself. It is a knowing of one's own strength, fortified by the mortal dangers of poverty, labor, misogyny, white supremacy. It is the Statue of Liberty looking a bully in the eye in a barroom and saying to someone standing behind her: 'Hold my torch.'"[122] That's an inspiring symbol of holding on to your own vision and not letting the attacks of petty-minded politicians wear her down. Maxine Waters is definitely one who has said, "hold my torch," and taken her gloves off. AOC has followed that path.

After leaving Kansas, Ocasio-Cortez stayed in the Midwest, stumping in Missouri for Cori Bush. She explained why it was so important to visit these places and meet people directly. "When someone actually knocks on your door or goes to your civic association meeting and you actually touch their hand, it really does change everything," said Ocasio-Cortez. She had found that out through direct experience, having walked the streets of the Bronx and Queens with such determination that she had worn holes in her shoes—something she showed off through a tweet bearing a photo of the beat-up shoes. "Respect the hustle," she tweeted. As a

122 Ibid.

natural-born politician, AOC knew that the same kind of door-to-door organizing is the basis for politics across the country and that people in different states and communities suffer the same kind of pain. "There are places in the Bronx and neighborhoods in Queens that look like neighborhoods in Wichita. I walked in thinking I was in for a world of hurt," she told Smarsh. "There is this impulse to just abandon it. To just say, you know what, forget it—it's a lost cause. It's just gonna be difficult or hurtful or dangerous. But I decided to go in anyway."[123]

Too many of the coastal elites don't bother to make a trip like that, even leaders of the Democratic Party who purport to speak for working families and vulnerable communities. Somehow, time in DC in the halls of power, on planes to key fund-raising locales like San Francisco and Martha's Vineyard, or at cocktail parties with high-living donors, causes them to forget to listen to the problems of people just scraping by. "Flyover country," that's the dismissive label slapped on wide swaths of middle America by many members of the ruling class, whether Democrats or Republicans. The fact that Trump paid attention to these people was one of the reasons he was able to appeal to them, despite his disinterest in actually helping them with the struggles they face. AOC and her approach to politics has upended how Democrats do business, with exciting results. As Democratic Senator Bernie Sanders said to *The Guardian*, "It is beyond comprehension, the degree to which the Democratic party nationally has essentially

123   Ibid.

abdicated half of the states in this country to rightwing Republicans, including some of the poorest states in America, those in the south. The reason I go to Kansas and many so-called red states is that I will do everything that I can to bring new people into the political process in states which are today conservative," Sanders said. "I do not know how you turn those states around unless you go there and get people excited."[124]

Naturally, the status quo is always easier. Searching for new voters or finding new and exciting candidates is dangerous. In March 2019, the division of the Party that raises money for House races, the Democratic Congressional Campaign Committee, made it known that it was blacklisting any consultants—media, fundraising, strategy, organizing, whatever capacity they serve a candidate—who had the temerity to provide services to any candidate running against a Democratic incumbent in a primary, no matter whether the seat is in a solidly Democratic district or a marginal one.[125]

But status quo thinking produces status quo results. There would still be a Democrat from the Queens-Bronx district if Crowley had won, but there would be not be a member of Congress from that area challenging the party to do better on climate change or economic justice or

124 Ibid.
125 Eliza Relman, "The Democratic Party is Cracking Down on Candidates Who Hope to Be the Next Alexandria Ocasio-Cortez, and Progressives are Fighting Back," *Business Insider,* April 20, 2019, https://www.businessinsider.com/democratic-party-primary-challengers-crackdown-2019-4.

student loans—or to steer clear of entanglements with Wall Street bankers and corporate donors. There would not be a fresh voice explaining the overly intimate relationship between lobbyists and legislative outcomes. And there would not be a young woman of color bringing new voters and new energy to the political process—and along the way, refreshing our understanding of what democracy is supposed to be. "We are for the status quo" does not win elections, let alone hearts and minds.

"We are for the status quo" does not change policy either. So when Alexandria Ocasio-Cortez and the other new progressive members arrived in Washington, they began to shake things up. The *Washington Post* styled it "Old Dem Caucus Meet New Dem Caucus."[126] Jacqueline Alemany, in her the Power Up column for the *Washington Post*, was admiring in her observations of how much influence the new cohort was having and so soon. "Just a few examples: the challenge to Pelosi once again assuming the speakership; the fights over Medicare-for-all and how the party plans to approach the Green New Deal. To be clear: these issues are still part of the new guard's wish list, and nothing has happened on the legislative front to make them reality. But there's no question the ideas themselves

126 Jacqueline Alemany, "Power Up: Alexandria Ocasio-Cortez and Company is Taking on the Old Guard. And They are Having Some Success," *Washington Post*, March 7, 2019, https://www. washingtonpost.com/news/powerpost/paloma/powerup/2019/03/07/ powerup-alexandria-cortez-ocasio-and-company-is-taking-on-the-old-guard-and-they-re-having-some-success/5c8036c41b326b2d177d5ffe/.

are agenda-setting and have moved the party leftward, as many 2020 candidates embrace them."[127]

One of the major reasons AOC and her allies "the Squad" have been able to have an impact that is outsized is that they are actually speaking for the Democratic base that has been frustrated by politicians who seem to listen more to lobbyists and donors than to their constituents and grassroots soldiers. What the Squad has done is listen to an engaged electorate, a Democratic base that is demanding change in how business is done in Washington. These are the people who might have stayed home in 2016 because they did not feel their votes would make a difference but were excited and optimistic in 2018. Part of their willingness to shake up the status quo is the Squad's commitment to advancing principled policy positions and not just getting ahead in politics. For all of us, this is a good lesson: remember your own reasons for doing what you do. People will listen when you voice your values. They may not agree, but they will listen and respect you for it.

The people who do the work for the party by knocking on doors, running phone banks, and making small donations have felt alienated by the party's failure to embrace policies that help them. Why has the Democratic Party pushed a free trade agenda that has undercut so many jobs in the United States? Why hasn't it endorsed a $15 minimum wage so that low-wage workers can get a bit of a leg up or free child care so families aren't strapped or

---

127 Ibid.

forced to provide their children with less-than-adequate care? Why haven't there been unanimous demands to end the tip credit for waiters and other tipped employees or to get rid of the special tax break for hedge fund managers? Well, because in Washington, special interests and the wealthy are closer to the ear of elected officials, and we have a campaign finance system that makes them inclined to listen. And the longer the elected officials spend in DC, the harder it becomes for them to hear the voices of those who don't attend the cocktail parties or eat at restaurants like The Palm. But the election of Donald Trump has pushed the Democratic base to ask for more—it's resonating and putting wind in the sails of the new members who have come to the capital city. What makes them—and AOC in particular—able to accomplish their goals is that they know that the status quo is neither a recipe for success nor for being true to one's self. That's a lesson for all of us.

With the issues she works on and how she talks about them, Ocasio-Cortez continues to challenge the powers that be and the accepted way of doing business in Washington and in New York City politics. AOC could have tried to step into Crowley's shoes and play the game with the old guard, to attend the same functions and meet the same Wall Street financiers to give money to her campaign. But she has not. Mostly, that's because she hasn't tried. But it's not clear she would have been welcomed into the charmed circle even if she had asked for admission. New York, like most places, has a strong old boys' network. The governor is the son of a governor. The mayor served first on the school board and then in other offices before taking over Gracie Mansion. The men who dominate the political class have worked their way up the ladder with the aid of other men, mostly white men, to ascend to the highest reaches. Would they have extended a hand to a young woman of Puerto Rican heritage? The answer is not at all clear. Michael Reich, an ally of her opponent, Joe Crowley, summed it up, perhaps inadvertently: "I wouldn't even know how to reach her, and she certainly hasn't reached out to me. She is on the national level, the international level, and I don't think she has any interest in the local level, frankly."[128] Still, there are some in the New York power structure who hope she will bring her star power and her energy inside the tent. Jay Jacobs, head of the state Democratic Party, wistfully suggested that remaining an "anti-establishment person" would not serve her interests in the long term. Better, Jacobs told *Politico*, would be for her to join forces. "She can still maintain her progressive position, but it would be more beneficial to what she wants to accomplish," he said.[129] But AOC knows that "progressive positions" often wilt when exposed to too much Wall Street money

---

128 David Freedlander, "How Alexandria Ocasio-Cortez Broke All the Rules of New York Politics," *Politico*, April 8, 2019, https://www.politico.com/magazine/story/2019/04/08/alexandria-ocasio-cortez-new-york-226578.

129 Ibid.

and to too many parties bankrolled by lobbyists and special interests.

Andrew Cuomo, New York's governor, tried to dismiss her as a unicorn, someone who benefited from low voter engagement and an absent incumbent who barely came to the district. He touted his own win in that same district in the governor's race to claim that AOC was not a harbinger of a new kind of politics.[130] But he was wrong. Cuomo no doubt, like many overconfident members of the old boys' club, assumed she would defer to the political elders on important political issues. One of those issues—Amazon's stated interest in setting up a satellite headquarters in Queens—showed that Congresswoman Ocasio-Cortez did not see it that way. Cuomo and other New York politicians had been making a play for Amazon's new home for a long time, hoping for a payoff in jobs and economic benefits as well as, no doubt, political patronage and increased lucre for the campaign coffers. Many residents, however, did not see Amazon's coming to town as a net win for New Yorkers. Besides the hefty subsidies New York would pay to the company, those people who live in the neighborhood close to the proposed site anticipated headaches with more people on the subway, more congestion in the streets, and higher rents. AOC, recognizing that many families in her district would see only the downside of having the behemoth as

---

130   Ibid.

a neighbor, called on her followers to fight the "creeping overreach of one of the world's biggest corporations."[131]

Amazon decided to seek another home.

It's hard to fathom how she does it. So many powerful people lined up against her before she won. So many powerful people willed her to fail after she was elected. So many powerful people expected her to conform if she did not in fact fail. It's an extreme version of what so many women face. Expected to follow the path of least resistance, of not causing trouble, of effacing yourself, many women do in fact comply. It's hard to be a rebel. But it's an important effort to make, in big ways or in small. Sometimes it is enough to decide that you are going to choose the paint color for your house or where you go for dinner. That daily practice of speaking your mind, exercising your willpower, makes you stronger for the decisions that control your life—what job to pursue, where to live, and how to be your best self.

Ocasio-Cortez has stayed clear of the entanglements of the traditional political hierarchy in New York and in Washington. More importantly, she has stayed true to the positions that made her campaign so inspiring to so

131 Aria Bendiz, "Amazon has canceled its New York City HQ2 plans. Here's why many New Yorkers opposed the project," *Business Insider*, February 14, 2019 https://www.businessinsider.com/why-new-yorkers-opposed-amazon-hq2-2019-2.

many young people, those whose economic security has been shaken by the gentrification of New York, and those who fear the negative consequences from a rapidly warming climate. Al Sharpton, the civil rights leader, MSNBC commentator, and political powerhouse in New York, recognized her willingness to walk her own path. "She is going to have to navigate and understand the differences and the various segments of the nation and this city," Sharpton said. "I have seen people blow up before. You have to make sure that you are firm in what you believe and that every exit ramp is leading to something and not a dead end."[132]

Challenging the status quo is hard. When I think about the times I have decided to defy conventional wisdom and try something new and different, I have worried about whether I was capable. For women and people of color who decide to pursue a dream that heretofore has been reserved for white people or men, not only do they worry about their own skills and capabilities but they also bear the burden of symbolizing whether women and people of color are qualified at all—that is, my failure or success will be judged by others to represent whether my group is worthy. That's a hard burden to carry. No white man serves as a symbol for all of his fellows; each gets to rise or fall on his own, without the

---

132   David Freedlander, "How Alexandria Ocasio-Cortez Broke All the Rules of New York Politics," *Politico,* April 8, 2019, https://www. politico.com/magazine/story/2019/04/08/alexandria-ocasio-cortez-new-york-226578.

added weight of disappointing a whole group of people or being pointed to as evidence that every such person is not ready, capable, smart enough, or deserving enough to do the job.

When I was a little girl, I loved to play baseball. It was just around the time that Little League had allowed girls to try out—after being forced to do so by a girl who was denied the opportunity and then sued. I really wanted to be part of a team, but I was too scared to put myself in that vulnerable situation. I knew the boys (and their fathers) didn't want me there. So I didn't try. I have always regretted that. But later in life, when I had the chance to apply to be chief of staff to US Senator Maria Cantwell, I went for it. As I mentioned, I was intimidated by the thought of becoming a Senate chief of staff but decided to throw my hat in the ring anyway.

The job pushed me to the limit, but I learned that I am in fact capable, that I have what it takes to make it in the boys' world. I also realized that there were more people on my side than against me. I discovered—or perhaps forged—a support network. If there's anything I have learned in the years since then it is that people of goodwill actually like giving advice and help. Rather than opening you up to criticisms of not knowing what you are doing, asking for advice can help you get on the right path quickly. By learning from the experiences of others, I avoided many mistakes and quickly put in place office policies that worked. I could have spent a lot of time cleaning up my own messes if I had not had this support network to assist me.

That's my philosophy now—follow your dreams and upend the status quo. And don't hesitate to ask for advice. I personally love to give advice.

It must be acknowledged that there's a lot of emotional and mental cost in pushing against boundaries, even if there's exhilaration and satisfaction in finding success.

But it is not just in challenging the old boys that AOC defies the status quo. She's also not afraid to demand more from her allies on the left. She has worked closely with groups like the Working Families Party (WFP) that seek to push Democrats to be more progressive. Even those groups, however, should not presume that AOC will defer to the traditional way of doing business—for example, she asked WFP to bring along "rank-and-file members" when the leaders meet with her and not assume that she should meet only with the higher-level people. With what sounded like sour grapes, one labor leader complained to *Politico*, "I didn't get the sense that she is interested in playing well with others." He continued, insinuating that AOC was making this request as a ploy to avoid harder conversations. "People have ways of doing things and I don't get the sense that she is interested in substantive questions if she doesn't want to meet us as individuals," he said.[133]

But WFP and other activist groups and individuals are learning that they can't expect AOC simply to conform to their expectations, because AOC and her brand of shake-it-up politics are not going anywhere. She has already helped to establish a new group to train campaign operatives to help in future elections. And her own group of stalwarts has continued to work with her and remain vocal in New York City politics—as in, for example, helping scuttle Amazon's plans to move to town. Some of the old guard are so rattled by this development and AOC's star power that they decided to move the congressional primaries so they are on the same date as the other state elections as a way to weaken challengers. There are even rumors that state leaders might change the district lines to make it harder for her to get reelected. But even that would probably not put an end to her career as a congresswoman. "No incumbent congressmember would want her drawn into their district," Bill Lipton, head of WFP in New York explained to *Politico*. "She's too popular and too good a campaigner. And the WFP and every progressive activist in the state will knock on doors day and night to ensure she's reelected."[134]

While challenging the "old boys" is hard, pushing

---

133   Ibid.

134   David Freedlander, "How Alexandria Ocasio-Cortez Broke All the Rules of New York Politics," *Politico*, April 8, 2019, https://www.politico.com/magazine/story/2019/04/08/alexandria-ocasio-cortez-new-york-226578.

your friends is harder, especially for women and people of color who are expected to defer to others when it comes to key decisions about strategy and tactics. When women or people of color speak up in meetings to give alternative views, these individuals are often talked over, ignored, or dismissed. Or, even more aggravating, it often happens that the points they make are stated later by someone else, white and male, and suddenly the salience and value of those ideas are recognized and applauded. Even their friends do this at times. And it is especially with friends that women are supposed to be nice and collegial, team-oriented and not confrontational. It is one thing for women or minorities to get elected, selected, or fight for leadership positions, but then when these individuals push for bold new policies like Medicare for All or a wealth tax, pushing for more than allies might want, they are told to back down. But it is exactly with allies and friends that they have to demand the most and to expect willingness to accept fresh ideas and approaches from new colleagues entering into positions of power.

Refusing to conform is not easy. It produces backlash and heartache, attacks and disparagement, blame and shame. Women are taught to try to please, so it is particularly difficult for us to face the onslaught of criticism that comes with being an iconoclast. But it is far worse when we realize that we have not been true to ourselves or our beliefs. How many of us have had that sickening feeling of thinking we have betrayed our own cause by going along with the conventional wisdom or by failing to speak up when a cherished value is undermined or a friend belittled? I say this not as an effort to make us feel more guilt or more shame but simply to say that, like working out, we usually feel better after the exertion of willpower to push back on the patriarchy. AOC can play the role of a beloved spin class instructor or favorite high school track coach by asking us to dig into our reserves of moral muscle and say and do the right thing, despite the pain or patronizing pushback.

So how do we learn to build that muscle? For me, it was a slow process—and one that hasn't ended—of learning how to follow my own compass. The first step is to determine what direction you want to go in. What exactly matters to you? Is it politics? Is it an issue that is being fought over that you care about? Is it a career that excites you, one in which you'd like to excel? Do you want to be the best friend and ally you can be or the best parent or mentor? Or are you working to help improve people's lives bit by bit, making a difference for individuals by helping them find jobs or learn skills or register to vote? Any and all of those goals are laudable and worth pursuing, if that's what you want to do. Once you have set your path, you have to practice cutting through the choppy seas that will try to push you back to shore. Winds will blow and gales will howl as those who think you should be doing something else block your path. But with every gust of criticism, you need to think about the alternative. What if I don't follow my own road map? What if I let myself get blown off course? In most cases, you will realize that for all the struggle, keeping on is better than caving in. And as I said, this involves "practice" because it is really true that "practice makes perfect." Or at least that practice makes it come easier the second, third, and fourth times you hear the negative remarks. You build up the muscle that shields your self-worth and self-confidence from the body blows of criticism. And at some point, you will be far enough down your chosen path that you will not care that some people may not approve. Some people will always be able to hurt you—the people you love, for example—but even they will have less power to slow you down or turn you around than they did. You too will be able to say "hold my torch."

For AOC, her critics are not just in New York City or even New York State. They range from the white ever-the-adolescent male gamers who covet her and hate her at the same time, the moderate Democrats who believe her existence is a challenge to their brand and pro-corporate ideology (it is), and the plutocrats who like the system just as it is, thank you very much. Democratic pollster John Anzalone argues that her effort to push the party leaders on climate change and political reform somehow doesn't show sufficient regard to his views. "My main gripe about AOC is that while I respect her voice in the party, I don't think she respects mine or anyone else's who differs with her on policy or comes from a different political electoral reality," he tweeted.[135] But since when

---

135   Chris Cilizza, "The Alexandria Ocasio-Cortez Backlash Begins," CNN, March 4, 2019, https://www.cnn.com/2019/03/04/politics/alexandria-ocasio-cortez-democratic-party-ideology/index.html.

does politics involve deferring to someone else's views? Isn't the idea that we argue and debate and hopefully come to an agreement about a policy we can all support? How can that work if advocates like AOC simply shut up? Isn't that what Anzalone is saying? "Wait your turn?" Or even more clearly, "please sit down."

At times, it can be dangerous to speak up. In late May 2019, fans at a minor-league baseball game in Fresno, California, were shown a video between games depicting "enemies of freedom." North Korean leader Kim Jong Un, former Cuban president Fidel Castro, and Ocasio-Cortez were all included in the video. The Fresno Grizzlies' fans saw a film that purported to honor veterans on Memorial Day and included a clip from President Ronald Reagan's first inaugural address as well as many images of soldiers and other patriotic themes. With the words of Reagan as backdrop—"As for the enemies of freedom, those who are potential adversaries, they will be reminded that peace is the highest aspiration of the American people,"—AOC's picture dominated the frame. "We will negotiate for it, sacrifice for it. We will not surrender for it, now or ever." She immediately got death threats. These types of media attacks generate immediate responses from violent and hating people. In response, AOC tweeted "What people don't (maybe do) realize is when orgs air these hateful messages, my life changes bc of the flood of death threats they inspire," she said. "I've had mornings where I wake up & the 1st thing I do w/ my coffee is review photos of the men (it's always men) who want to kill me." The baseball club, a farm team for the Washington Nationals, expressed surprise and alarm that somehow such a video had eluded internal controls.[136]

In another example, the Ohio Federation of College Republicans used AOC's image on an email designed to raise money, with a subject line that Ocasio-Cortez is "a domestic terrorist." Immediately, she faced more death threats and a need to alert the Capitol Police. According to AOC, "This puts me in danger every time." It is daunting to face that kind of headwind—not just the taunts, denigration, and dismissal but threats of violence. And let's be clear: women face greater dangers when they challenge the status quo. They are a double threat, looking to upend existing power hierarchies but also gender roles. When such women are public figures, the danger and threats of violence are increased. That's what Alexandria Ocasio-Cortez now faces every day of her life. But she persists.

When Elizabeth Warren was being criticized for having practiced law while a professor at Harvard (something many law professors do), not because she represented clients whose interests were adverse to her stated political beliefs but because she actually charged them for her work (unbelievable! How could she?), a commentator on Twitter remarked that Ocasio-Cortez had been criticized

---

136 Marisa Iati and Reis Thebault, "Ocasio-Cortez responds to baseball team's 'enemies of freedom' Memorial Day video," *The Washington Post*, May 28, 2019, https://www.washingtonpost.com/sports/2019/05/28/ocasio-cortez-featured-among-americas-enemies-freedom-baseball-teams-memorial-day-video/?utm_term=.678e65ea512b&wpisrc=nl_politics-pm&wpmm=1.

as not ready for elected office because as a waitress she hadn't earned enough. "The people who belittle @AOC for being a former waitress are the same faulting @ewarren for billing out at $675/hr. So how much exactly should world-changing women make?" tweeted Katherine M. Gordon.[137] AOC retweeted, adding, "The reason women are critiqued for being too loud or too meek, too big or too small, too smart to be attractive or too attractive to be smart, is to belittle women out of standing up publicly. The goal is to 'critique' into submission. & That applies to anyone challenging power."[138] AOC's right-on reply prompted another woman to tweet, "The system, from the beginning, was set up to put a woman in her place, a place that was comfortable for men, and to keep her there. We will no longer submit to such critiques. We are women, hear us roar!"[139]

Even for those who disagree with her views on specific issues, AOC's ability to shine a light on areas where Democrats have diverged from their values should be refreshing.

Teen Vogue rightly celebrates the AOC way—not letting the haters get you down but following your dream with a smile on your face. Yet her dancing was not the only action that got props from *Teen Vogue*. The magazine

137   Katherine M. Gordon, Twitter, May 27, 2019, https://twitter.com/katgordon/status/1133199021940461569.
138   Alexandria Ocasio-Cortez, Twitter, May 28, 2019, https://twitter.com/AOC/status/1133383123503321090.
139   Angela Belcamino, Twitter, May 28, 2019, https://twitter.com/AngelaBelcamino/status/1133403469203877888.

also enthused that AOC "attended the January 3 swearing-in ceremony in Washington, DC in a white pantsuit, paying homage to the pioneering women who paved the way before her. From the women of the suffrage movement to Shirley Chisholm, the first black woman elected to Congress in 1968 who also wore white to her ceremony, AOC's historic references run deep." In the article, *Teen Vogue* celebrated both her policy positions and her white pantsuit. She is both chic and sharp intellectually, a smarty-pants and a fashion plate. Her red lipstick, she said, was in honor of Justice Sonia Sotomayor, who like AOC hails from the Bronx. Sotomayor, the first Latinx to serve on the Supreme Court, chose bright red nail polish for her confirmation hearing in defiance of White House urging to tone it down.

AOC, along with the cohort of young women newly elected to Congress, has not ceased to express herself, through her clothes, her tweets, and her policies. She's showing, wrote *Teen Vogue*, that in order to disrupt the status quo, one must stay true to oneself. The women newly elected to the 116th Congress are cognizant of the impact of their wardrobe choices.

As AOC is quoted in the piece, "Next time someone tells Bronx girls to take off their hoops, they can just say they're dressing like a Congresswoman."[140]

---

140   Roberta Gorin-Paracka, "Rep. Alexandria Ocasio-Cortez Explains Why She Wore Red Lipstick and Gold Hoop Earrings to Swearing-In Ceremony, " *Teen Vogue*, January 5, 2019, https://www.teenvogue.com/story/alexandria-ocasio-cortez-red-lipstick-gold-hoop-earrings-swearing-in-ceremony.

So for all of the rest of us, the next time someone tells us to take off our hoops, dress differently, talk more softly, or remain silent, we can just say, "we are acting like a Congresswoman." Be yourself, follow your dreams, and shake things up.

CHAPTER FIVE

Stand by Your Friends

WHAT COULD BE MORE THREATENING to the patriarchy than a strong woman? And several strong women—that's a revolution! Obviously, that can't be tolerated. One way to thwart this challenge to the prevailing hierarchy is to denigrate women who speak up or who dare to have opinions; another way is to divide them from each other.

While she doesn't hesitate to challenge established conventions, AOC is fiercely loyal to her friends and allies. When fellow freshman congresswoman Ilhan Omar was attacked for making remarks about Israel some called anti-Semitic, AOC used her media presence to call out the critics. "It's not my position to tell people how to feel, or that their hurt is invalid," she tweeted. "But incidents like these do beg the question: where are the resolutions against homophobic statements? For anti-blackness? For xenophobia? For a member saying he'll 'send Obama home to Kenya?'" She also posted that "one of the things that is hurtful about the extent to which reprimand is sought of Ilhan is that no one seeks this level of reprimand when members make statements about Latinx + other communities." And she underscored the hypocrisy of those attacking Omar who had not similarly raised concern when Republican Jason Smith yelled on the House floor "go back to Puerto Rico" at Rep. Tony Cárdenas. AOC made it clear to Democratic leaders that an attack on Omar that accused her of anti-Semitism but didn't call out anti-Muslim slurs or other discriminatory language would not fly. Her broadside against those Democrats who immediately followed the Republican lead to chastise Omar resulted in a change to the resolution that had been introduced to chastise Omar. Once drafted only to focus on Omar's words, which many believe were twisted to mean something she didn't intend, the final resolution introduced by Speaker Pelosi was redrafted to focus on hate more generally.[141]

Donald Trump and the Republicans doubled down in attacking Omar during the hot summer of 2019.

---

141   Mike DeBonis and Rachael Bade, "House Democrats Leaders Move to Broaden Anti-Semitism Resolution to Deal with Other Religious Bigotry," *The Washington Post,* March 5, 2019, https://www.washingtonpost.com/powerpost/ocasio-cortez-defends-omar-criticizes-democrats-over-anti-semitism-resolution/2019/03/05/f05ae738-3f56-11e9-922c-64d6b7840b82_story.html?utm_term=.050c840f94a4.

Accusing her of hating America and hating Israel, Trump tweeted that she and the three other members of "the Squad"—AOC, Ayanna Pressley, and Rashida Tlaib—should "go back" to the countries "they came from." All, of course, are citizens, and all but Omar were born in the United States, but that's of no matter to the truth-defying president. It was enough that they served as a useful foil to rev up his racist base. He even led them in chants of "send them back" at rallies he held soon after the exchange of tweets.[142] Not easily intimidated, even when directly attacked by the president of the United States, the four friends stood together. At a press conference, the four women rejected Trump's assertion that somehow disagreeing with him and his cruel policies equates with a hatred of America. "This is simply a disruption and a distraction from the callous, chaotic, and corrupt culture of this administration," Pressley said. AOC added, "We don't leave the things that we love, and when we love this country, what that means is that we propose the solutions to fix it."[143] That's always been the way of patriots in the United States, those who fought to eradicate slavery from our land, who fought to give women the vote, and who continue the battle for economic fairness and against

---

142 Oliver Darcy, "Media react to 'send her back' chant at Trump rally," CNN, July 17, 2017, https://www.cnn.com/2019/07/17/media/donald-trump-north-carolina-rally-reliable-sources/index.html

143 Matt McNulty, "Meet 'The Squad': The Four Democratic Congresswomen of Color Trump Blasted in Racist Tweets," *People,* July 17, 2019, https://people.com/politics/meet-aoc-the-squad-ilhan-omar-rashida-tlaib-ayanna-pressley/.

discrimination. In attacking the women, Trump did something that Democratic Party leaders had not been able to do—unify its members in defending the Squad and rebuking the racist rants of the president.

In defending Omar and other allies, AOC uses the tools that have made her strong to push back on the trolls. She's got a commanding presence on social media, particularly on Twitter, and it has been said that she has "as much social media clout as her fellow freshmen Democrats combined." As of February 2019, she has 3.1 million Twitter followers, far more than Speaker of the House Nancy Pelosi. With more than two million Instagram followers and half a million on Facebook, she's positioned to defend her friends and her ideas—and she does. She is a living demonstration of the truth that women stand up for each other and exposes the fake news of catfights and competitiveness.

Even when they are ambitious and strong, women can also be warm and caring, nurturing even. They are our mothers who we turn to when we are sad and need a shoulder to cry on. They are our BFFs with whom we can share our relationship problems or small triumphs. They are our daughters, nieces, and friends' kids who grow up to be strong and determined young women. Women's friendship is famous for being life-sustaining. I say this from personal experience, but it is also a documented fact:

The psychology behind strong female friendships is strong. According to a study published in the *Journal of Clinical Oncology*, women with early-stage breast cancer were four times more likely to die from cancer if they didn't have very many friends. Those with a larger group of friends with early-stage breast cancer had a much better survival rate. This beneficial effect of friendship was felt whether the friends lived near or far.[144]

One of the many unfortunate tropes about women is that they are "catty" and that they stab each other in the back. We all know the way that society describes men as leaders and women as "bossy." That men are strong but women are "pushy." But we also are denigrated in how we interact with each other: men can have a debate or an argument; women have a catfight or bitch fest. Men can decide to exclude a former pal because they no longer get along; women are mean girls. The most popular guy in school is an alpha male; the young women are "queen bees."

There are so many well-known stories—from Betty and Veronica to Jennifer Aniston and Angelina Jolie to *Real Housewives of Beverly Hills* and *The Bachelor*. Over and over we hear about women hating women. We all know, however, that women are actually friends with other women! In fact, for many women, their best friends

---

144 Kristen Fuller, "The Importance of Female Friendships Among Women," *Psychology Today*, August 16, 2018 https://www. psychologytoday.com/us/blog/happiness-is-state-mind/201808/ the-importance-female-friendships-among-women.

are often other women. They stand by them and help them in times of trouble. They lift them up when they are down and celebrate them when they are up. There's even research that shows that when women are in positions of power, they add many more women to the leadership positions.[145] So why is there this mythology about women and their "catfights?"

New York Times contributor Kayleen Schaefer writes, "There is a word that starts with 'c' that is exclusively used to describe women. Usually, it's deployed when we are being argumentative, standing up for ourselves, or otherwise not behaving as nicely as we're expected to. It's especially targeted at women in politics." With several women running for the Democratic Party's nomination for president in 2018 and 2019, commentators worried that the word would be used to try to knock some of them out of the race. Caroline Heldman, who runs the organization The Representation Project, which works to address this type of coded language, told Schaefer that calling a disagreement between women a "catfight" was a way to deliberately undermine women candidates. "It's such a good diminutive label. It suggests the fight isn't a real fight, but more important, catfights exist to titillate heterosexual men. It reduces female presidential candidates to not-serious contenders," she said. Exactly right.

---

145   David A. Matsa and Amalia R. Miller, "Chipping Away at the Glass Ceiling: Gender Spillovers in Corporate Leadership," *RAND Working Paper No. WR-842*, April 3, 2011, https://papers.ssrn.com/sol3/papers.cfm?abstract_id=1799575.

And it reduces female interactions to competition and caterwauling.[146] Women can both disagree and debate in substantive and cordial ways but also can be friends and mutual supporters, serious opponents as well as significant allies.

AOC has not come to the defense of her female friends just since she became known to the public. Her fierceness has characterized her approach to friendship and loyalty for a lifetime. Writer Ryan Grim described a particularly nauseating #MeToo moment of female objectification that happened while Ocasio-Cortez was tending bar at Coffee Shop, a trend-forward restaurant that claimed chic waitstaff and mediocre food. AOC's boss at the restaurant asked all his waitstaff to line up so he could decide which was the best-looking and then assign the sections of the restaurant, giving the best ones to the women he deemed most attractive. That crossed a line for Ocasio-Cortez, who in turn quit. According to Grim, "It took a charm offensive and a set of apologies from the owners, along with a promise the 'contest' would never be repeated, for AOC to agree to come back to work." On Twitter, AOC gave some more context to this story, saying that the situation still bothered her. Grim quoted her tweet, in which she said "'What's wild is that I'm a member of Congress & I STILL found myself pausing at this, scared of possible repercussions of this

---

146 Kayleen Schaefer, "Me-OW! It's the End of the Catfight," *New York Times*, April 24, 2019, https://www.nytimes.com/2019/04/24/style/is-the-word-catfight-sexist.html.

story being public. Imagine how everyday waitresses feel,' she said."[147] Coffee Shop closed down in 2018.

I, too, have waited tables and I know how many indignities waiters face. And I have heard many stories from other women about managers telling them to wear tighter shirts and of customers asking for drinks with sexed-up names just so they could ask the female server to repeat them. Some of the feedback I've gotten from customers: "Is that my orgasm?" "Can you give me my orgasm please?" "Sex on the beach, is that what you are giving me?" Fortunately for me, I did not actually have to wait tables for too long—each time, it was a stopgap while I was looking for something else. But it was long enough for me to have real lived experience of the low wages and high incidence of sexual harassment in the restaurant industry. We often think of #MeToo as a phenomenon of Hollywood—the "casting couch"—or other professional settings. But vulnerable workers are just that, vulnerable in all ways. When a woman is dependent on a job because she has no savings, is a single mom, owes rent, needs medications, is caring for an elderly parent, or is otherwise strapped, she has little ability to push back. Even for Ocasio-Cortez, her anxiety at challenging her boss and then quitting a job that paid the rent is still palpable. That existential fear is why so few women in these kinds of jobs are able to push back on harassment and degrading behavior. Marginal women fear falling over the edge.

---

147   Blast email from Ryan Grim to his listserv.

That's why it is so important for women to protect other women, like AOC did with her friends. And that's why groups like the Restaurant Opportunities Center (ROC) and the National Domestic Workers Association are so vital. They both bring needed attention to the harm inflicted on these women and provide a support network. AOC continues to fight to raise the minimum wage and tends bar at fund-raisers to do so. She doesn't forget her friends.

As I wrote in my book *Under the Bus*, "Minimum-wage workers are seriously underpaid, but tipped employees may have it the worst. They are a subcategory of minimum-wage workers in which women make up an even higher percentage of the workforce." Under the Fair Labor Standards Act, tipped employees are "those who customarily and regularly receive more than $30 per month in tips. Tips are the property of the employee. The employer is prohibited from using an employee's tips for any reason other than as a credit against its minimum wage obligation to the employee ('tip credit') or in furtherance of a valid tip pool. Only tips received by the employee may be counted in determining whether the employee is a tipped employee and in applying the tip credit."[148] But it often doesn't work out that way, as employers take tips from the tipped employees or fail to add to their wages if tips plus base wage fail to equal the minimum wage. It's a tough way to make a living, and

---

148   Caroline Fredrickson, *Under the Bus* (The New Press: New York: 2015), at p. 74.

very hard for workers, especially vulnerable women, to enforce their rights.

AOC and the ROC are working together on an effort to push for a higher federal minimum wage and an end to reduced wages for tipped employees, including putting AOC back behind the bar mixing drinks for the cause. In late May of 2019, AOC tweeted enthusiastically about her return to the role of mixologist: "To the silver spoon classists saying they're going to 'make AOC bartend again': You're in luck! I'll be bartending in NY-14 this week to promote a national living wage."

Ocasio-Cortez did not, however, forget why she was back behind the bar, calling her followers to action: "Now let's pass #RaiseTheWage and get $15 an hour minimum for every worker in America." And she also correctly noted that the $2.13 tipped wage is not a wage, it is "indentured servitude."

Far too few Americans understand the reality of making $2.13 per hour and depending on tips to bring up earnings to the full minimum wage, but fortunately for those who have experienced it, they have an ally in AOC. One of the reasons sexual harassment is so rampant in the restaurant industry is that supervisors, fellow waiters, and clients all know that the women working behind the bar or hoisting plates of food can't protest without losing a key part of their income or losing their job entirely. Women are expected to accept the pinches on the ass, the hands brushing their breasts "by accident," or the insulting comments as necessary accompaniment to any tip. If she objects or pushes the hand away vigorously, the small tip turns into 25 cents. Or nothing at all.

So that's why it is so important to raise the minimum wage and get rid of the tipped credit. Making the job of waiting tables or mixing drinks one that pays a living wage on its own without tips would mean that those workers would not have to bite their tongues when subject to life-crushing harassment or sexual assault. It would enable them to stand up for their legal right to be free of this type of discrimination on the job without fear of losing wages. And it would mean the difference for many between a life on the brink of poverty and a somewhat more solid hold on the ladder of economic security. But until then, it's important that we look to AOC as a model and speak out for those women tending bar, waiting tables, and cutting hair in support of fair wages and decent treatment. Because that's what friends are for.

When Ocasio-Cortez speaks about her friends, it's not just to defend but also to celebrate. As women, we also need to support and encourage each other in our successes, not just offer comfort when things go wrong. AOC seems to truly revel in the strong women who serve with her in Congress. Another member of the House, Pramila Jayapal, has been the subject of AOC's enthusiastic tweeting. Ocasio-Cortez recognizes other women's brilliance, such as in this tweet where she referenced a video of Jayapal explaining health-care issues: "Reminder that @RepJayapal already took everyone to school on #MedicareForAll. Watching how Pres candidates speak about healthcare really tells you who's studied these proposals + who hasn't. How much is Medicare for All? LESS than our current system. Rep. Pramila Jayapal @ RepJayapal #MedicareforAll spending is in the news a lot lately, but what do we currently spend on our health care system? I'm breaking it down."[149]

AOC celebrates not just her fellow elected officials but also the staff and advocates who work so hard behind the scenes. She makes it clear that the work she gets done, she does with the help of many others—and she trumpets that to the public and not just in behind-the-scenes thank-yous to her employees. For example, in a thread on Twitter, AOC showed how she shares credit where credit is due. She first described how she was able to pull off such a powerful performance at a hearing on the drug companies only because of the hard work of her staff. "A 23 y/o staffer in my office met w/ local HIV advocates. They argued the CDC held the patent for PrEP & Gilead was price gouging. She picked it up + dug in." The staffperson made sure the story was verifiable and then brought it to AOC, and they then worked with committee staff on how to introduce the information at the hearing. Because the Committee Chairman, Elijah Cummings (D-Md), supported the approach, AOC and her staff were able to make a difference. She proudly tweeted that as a result of the hearing, "PrEP is going generic a year early. It was thanks to: - Everyday people who advocated

---

149 Alexandria Ocasio-Cortez, Twitter, June 2, 2019, https:// twitter.com/search?q=AOC%20%40RepJayapal%20took%20everyone %20to%20school%20%23MedicareforAll%20&src=typed_query.

& didn't quit until someone listened - A young staffer who listened & dug in - Committee staff that took her seriously - Generous leadership that cultivates the next gen."[150]

She concluded her tweet thread by making sure her friends, allies, and constituents know that they all matter in the fight for good policy. "It ALL started with everyday people. You would really be surprised how much work here gets started because a journalist picked up on a story, or advocates organized people to command notice of an issue. It's inspiring how much power everyday people have. We just need to use it."

What people often fail to realize is that this kind of support is actually self-serving. For a boss, sticking up for good employees, paying them well, and thanking them for hard work well done, is really meaningful. It helps reduce staff turnover, keeps morale high, reduces stress, breeds loyalty, and makes outcomes stronger. All that is good for the company, office, organization, or other institution. It's a virtuous circle, which is definitely good for the workers but also for their savvy bosses who know that giving help and support redounds to the giver. It's an important life lesson.

One of her followers called her "a light in the darkness," for having acknowledged her staff.[151] I can attest from my experience on the Hill how rare that truly is.

150 Alexandria Ocasio-Cortez, Twitter, May 24, 2019, https://twitter.com/AOC/status/1131916272441208834.
151 Jacki Leach, Twitter, May 24, 2019, https://twitter.com/Book_Hog1/status/1131928310743592960.

While I certainly know of some members of Congress who remain conscious that they are only as good as their staff, few of them express their gratitude publicly for all the hard work that gets done behind the scenes. I say this not to suggest that members do not put in their hours—being an elected representative is grueling—but only to remind them and others that for a politician to be able to give a speech, attend a hearing and ask thoughtful questions, meet with several different groups of constituents and work on drafting legislation—all in one day!—requires a lot of people's help. As Hillary Clinton said, "it takes a village." To make the village successful, the villagers need to be thanked every once in a while. That they are not explains why there is such a high turnover on Capitol Hill.

Refreshingly, when members of Congress began to discuss a plan for lifting a freeze on congressional pay, stuck for a long time without an increase, Ocasio-Cortez broadened that to include staff, who are routinely paid much less than what they might earn if they weren't on Capitol Hill. And AOC used the news hook about congressional salaries to remind people that low-wage workers are really the ones who have the most need. "I see members all the time, I see the financial pressure that they're under because this job is unique," she said. "Members of Congress, retail workers—everybody should get a cost of living increase to accommodate for the changes in our economy."[152] She elaborated in an interview with the

---

152   Emily Cochrane, "A Truce Falters, and a Plan to Raise Congress's Pay Falls Apart," *New York Times,* June 11, 2019, https://www.nytimes .com/2019/06/11/us/politics/congress-pay-raise.html.

Washington Post, stating that "We should be fighting for pay increases for every American worker. We should be fighting for a $15 minimum wage, pegged to inflation. So that everybody in the United States with a salary, with a wage, gets a cost-of-living increase—members of Congress, retail workers, everybody."

She also made sure to explain that the staff turnover was in large part a result of the low pay.[153] Being on congressional staff is an amazing experience but also exhausting. And with the combination of long hours, high stress, and less than competitive pay scales, many senior staff drift away to more comfortable K Street offices to become lobbyists. They tell themselves that they will continue to help progressive leaders by raising money, by looking for nonprofit clients, for helping with policy ideas. AOC recognizes that all workers deserve a living wage and that staff as well as members of Congress should get cost-of-living increases if those are necessary to make the job livable to keep talented, committed people from leaving. Some people will still go off to K Street—congressional salaries will never compete with those of the private sector—but if the jobs pay decently and staff is treated well, the ones who matter will stay.

I spent almost ten years laboring on Capitol Hill and

153   Paul Kane, "Divergent pleas for pay raise from veteran lawmaker and freshman hit political hurdle," *The Washington Post*, June 11, 2019, https://www.washingtonpost.com/powerpost/divergent-pleas-for-pay-raise-from-veteran-lawmaker-and-freshman-hit-political-hurdle/2019/06/11/97f1eada-8c57-11e9-b08e-cfd89bd36d4e_story.html?utm_term=.4595968c138d.

have fond memories of my time there, but not a lot of them include moments when the senator or representative recognized the contributions of their staff. The fact is that staff make things happen, but many members of Congress don't seem to recall that when it comes time to take credit. I put in long, long hours and most of the time felt that I was proud to be doing that work—even if I was tired, missed my family, or really had hoped for a vacation, I knew my job was important and that I was contributing to the greater good of the nation through my public service. But for a few more members of Congress to remark on that and express gratitude would have gone a long way. That is why I cherish a memory I have of Senator Paul Wellstone, who died too young in a plane crash in Minnesota while home campaigning for reelection. I was sitting in the Democratic Cloak Room, which is an area for the senators just off the Senate floor. It was late at night and the Senate was having one of its "votaramas" when the senators vote on a whole series of amendments usually designed to frame a political issue for campaign attack ads, rather than to actually change the underlying bill. I had sat down on the sofa to rest for a few minutes when Senator Wellstone sat down beside me. "Why are you here?" he asked me. He didn't mean, "why are you, a staffer, sitting in the senators' cloakroom?" but rather "what brought you into politics?" I was confused. No one (no politician, I should say) had ever asked me what drove me and why I had taken this path. We sat and talked for a while. He was actually interested in my answers and hearing my personal story. I suppose it seems a small thing, but it felt enormous to me. Staff are invisible on the Hill until someone has to bear the blame for a glitch or a failure. Easily blamed, easily forgotten. It's a challenging career. And so when AOC recognizes the staff's contribution to her work as well as their need to be considered in any pay increase on Capitol Hill, that also seems enormous. It is as if Paul Wellstone was looking over her shoulder and smiling.

So defend your friends and celebrate their successes, but also remember to thank those who contribute to your own victories. That's the AOC way.

There's another trope about women besides that they are "catty," and that's that they don't help each other. They are described as competitive and backstabbing. The reality, though, is something different. Just as there are many men who are driven and aggressive and who stop at nothing to get ahead—though they are simply called "ambitious"—there are some women who behave this way. But just as there's an "old boys' network," so too do women help each other, mentor each other, and establish a virtuous circle of support that has helped many women, as well as men, get a leg up in a career, or at school, or in another activity. I certainly have been the beneficiary of this type of support, from the women who gave me recommendations for jobs, or helped coach me on applications or to prepare for interviews, from law professors who have remained friends and mentors and high school track coaches who gave me confidence and motivation. I have asked many women for advice about how to handle different challenges that have arisen on the job, whether that has been internal personnel and management issues or external questions about working with coalition partners or the media. They have been there for me at every step in my career, a supportive web of insights and information, consultation and confirmation, and criticism when warranted.

Similarly, I am truly committed to paying it forward. I do enjoy the role of mentor and counselor, so I can't claim to be self-sacrificing or saintly in any way. Nonetheless, it is a time commitment to provide ideas and connections to job seekers and others contemplating life changes, whether that's education or a career switch. But it is time worth spending because the rewards are great. I find real satisfaction in seeing where these mentees end up and how much they accomplish—and I can take a small bit of credit for that, which is a source of enjoyment. You help make the world a better place not only through your own actions but also through your legacy of helping others use their talents to change the world.

A great example of the "old girls' network" at work is something that one of my friends, Lori Andrus, helped to start—Emerge America. It's an organization dedicated to helping Democratic women run for office and giving them serious tools and support to do so. Many women in positions of power have already graduated from its program, and they turn around and help others. For example, the mayor of Oakland, California, Libby Schaaf, is one such graduate. When she needed a director of public safety, she turned to Venus Johnson, another graduate. While California is the home base, Emerge America "is currently training women in 17 states to run for offices up and down the ballot. This training is at the core of what we need to reinvigorate the women's movement—a focus on political power and strong female mentorship," states the group's website. And that could not be more true. The value of role models like AOC or Libby Schaaf for women is incalculable. They help us all understand not only that we can do it, but there are many women there to help us achieve our goals. According to Emerge, "When you run and win elected office, you have a responsibility to reach behind you and help the next woman up. Women supporting, mentoring, and guiding other women through the ranks is the only way that we will see parity in politics, or any industry for that matter." Venus Johnson imbibed that message from her training, and turned around on her first day on the job to give the job of police chief to another woman. That makes Oakland a city with six of its highest offices held by women.[154] It's a story of how standing up for your friends, helping women, and building political power all go together. Emerge has many more stories, but what is most important to remember is that women

---

154 "Building the Old Girls Network," Emerge America, accessed August 16, 2019, https://emergeamerica.org/building-old-girls-network/.

helping women is how we change America—and help ourselves. AOC has demonstrated her support in so many ways for other women who are in politics or want to enter the fray. From members of her "squad," to more senior mentors like Pramila Jayapal, to those running for office like Tiffany Caban, she shares credit, defends them from attacks, and gives them props when they might be overlooked.

In 2012, Michelle Obama said at the Democratic National Convention, "When you've worked hard, and done well, and walked through that doorway of opportunity, you do not slam it shut behind you. You reach back, and you give other folks the same chances that helped you succeed."[155]

Women helping women will change the world. AOC gets that—and that women need to be supported once they actually get the job and win the election. Her willingness to speak up for her newly elected colleagues has been a significant means to ensure that the Republicans aren't successful at denigrating them and at isolating them from the other Democrats. Divide and conquer is the strategy often used against courageous women, but other women can help prevent it from being successful.

A very useful way of internalizing a mutually supportive approach to women's relationships is by adopting the "shine theory." According to writer Meryl Williams,

---

155 Transcript: Michelle Obama's Convention Speech, NPR, September 4, 2012, https://www.npr.org/2012/09/04/160578836/transcript-michelle-obamas-convention-speech.

shine theory dictates that when you encounter a successful and impressive woman, you resist any feelings of envy or competition but instead decide to engage them, to get to know them, and to become friends. The idea is to recognize that one woman's shine doesn't make another woman dull, but actually helps her with her own glow. Williams wrote, "It's the idea that strong and powerful women make great friends, because they want to help other women they admire succeed—not take them down."[156] AOC has fully embraced this positive approach. Per her tweet that was included in Williams's blog: "Impostor syndrome isn't an internal issue. It's one that can be encouraged externally. It's not delusional to think you're undeserving, even if you've overcome great odds, when some stand to benefit from casting you as such. That's why we lift each other's light. #ShineTheory https://t.co/GYY26Zil3X."

Williams did something we should all do—she decided to live shine theory, to learn how to fully adopt it as her guiding ethos. So she went out of her way to celebrate and support successful women and to suppress her competitive feelings and envy. In her career as well as her hobbies she worked to live up to the ideal—and it was satisfying and actually made her happy. She detailed how in every area of her life—work, hobbies, her social networks—she endeavored to let shine theory govern

---

156 Meryl Williams, "AOC just tweeted about something called "shine theory"—here's what that is," *HelloGiggles,* January 11, 2019, https://hellogiggles.com/love-sex/friends/shine-theory/.

her interactions. Her career and working environment both improved as she consistently operated to appreciate the talents and drive of other women. For example, she writes about another reporter who worked for a different publication whom she would frequently encounter at events they had both been assigned to cover. "Instead of competing in a rivalry, we eventually started talking and realized we had a lot in common. We became friends, and when her company was looking for freelancers, she came to me first with the scoop." Similarly, she started to recognize how to work better with her boss, making sure to recognize each other's contributions to a successful project. She found that her work experience improved dramatically, with a better "work/life balance" as part of that. And in her efforts to become a better writer, she joined a group of other women to critique each other's work in a constructive way. Williams recognized how discouraging it can be for someone, especially a woman, starting out to get criticism on her writing. It's a challenge to make sure that the writing—or other work we all do— gets feedback that helps us improve what is delivered in a way that is constructive and doesn't tear us down. At the end of her blog, Williams concluded, "I'm sure you've got some stories of your own in which shine theory came into play. It's no secret: A rising tide lifts all boats.[157]

A rising tide does indeed lift all boats. When women are kind to and supportive of other women, it helps each of us—because we feel helped, but we also feel better

---

157 Ibid.

about ourselves when we do it for others. And we can also put wind in the sails of change for all women by guaranteeing we have systems in place that ensure workplaces and educational institutions serve women, that they don't allow harassment or discrimination, and where women are paid equally and traditional caregiving roles are valued and fairly compensated. For example, why should it be so hard to fulfill more than one role—worker and family member? Not to say it is easy for men, but for women we have still not put in place systems that allow parenting and working to coexist comfortably. It's a struggle. Some of us, who set policies for workplaces, can help establish practices that make the load a little lighter for parents and caregivers: paid family leave, flexible working hours, remote work possibilities, child care assistance, and so on. I have done that when I have been the decider on employment policies—and so has AOC.

Early on in her term, Ocasio-Cortez had a staffer go out on maternity leave. That happens a lot on Capitol Hill, but, unlike most staffers, Ariel Eckblad had twelve weeks of paid leave. And the legislative director wasn't worried about losing her job by using her benefits because she had a boss, AOC, who was fully supportive of her taking the time—despite the fact that she had just been elected to Congress and things were in full swing. Two other staffers were also expecting children, all of this on a tiny staff that gets tested to the limit every day. Unfortunately, the current family leave statute is completely inadequate because it does not mandate paid leave. The twelve weeks of unpaid leave under the law are available only to workers at larger companies. And even when women are eligible, many choose not to take the unpaid leave because they can't afford to go without wages for so long. While some employees get paid leave, ironically, well-paid men are the ones most likely to have that benefit. According to several labor economists, "Losing a day's pay is a real hardship for many families. If a low-wage worker making $10 an hour has a family of two children and misses more than three days of work without paid leave, the family would fall below the poverty line due to lost wages. Moreover, workers with less education—who are also more likely to be in low-paying jobs—suffer disproportionately when they are forced to choose between lost wages or their caregiving responsibilities."

AOC is one member of Congress who knows that congressional staff are not highly paid and that Washington, DC, is a very expensive city. Expecting staff to take unpaid leave makes it financially impossible for many new parents, and especially women, to stay home as long as they would like or need—and some cannot stay home at all, often with negative physical and mental consequences for mother and child. Recognizing that even small employers can work out processes to deal with colleagues out on leave, AOC has made sure to have a paid leave policy to enable staff from the most junior on up to be able to use it. If it is not a usable benefit, it is just window dressing. Some states are beginning to offer paid leave, and members of Congress have introduced legislation to add pay to the FMLA, so there is some sign of progress. President Trump has proposed six weeks of paid leave—although with him the devil is in the details.[158]

Jezebel interviewed Ocasio-Cortez's legislative director to better understand how AOC was implementing the policy in the office. According to Eckbald, AOC wanted to hire her, and the pregnancy was not going to interfere. "I was seven months pregnant when I joined the team and it was actually a great concern for me, the idea of joining the team and then after probably four to eight weeks, depending on when I delivered, leaving," Eckblad explained. "The representative said to me, explicitly, 'Listen, if you don't want to take the job because of what the work will be or because of the substance, that's fine. But if you're not taking the job because you're pregnant, I don't accept that. We will find a way to make it work, we will find a way to make sure that we have talented people on our team that also have families.' She wanted to figure out how to make that possible."

I fully support that approach. I too have hired very pregnant people, knowing they would go out on leave soon after joining the team. But I wanted both to have the very best, most suitable, and enthusiastic person for the job—and I also believe in paid leave, so I had no compunctions about having my new colleague immediately

158 Tracy Clark-Flory, "'People Rise to the Occasion,' How Alexandria Ocasio-Cortez's Office Makes an 'Unusual' Parental Leave Policy Work," *Jezebel*, June 13, 2019, https://theslot.jezebel.com/people-rise-to-the-occasion-how-alexandria-ocasio-cort-1835415040.

take advantage of it. It is beneficial not just for the individual, the child and the family, but for the office culture, the workforce, and for society at large. As Eckblad recounted to *Jezebel*, people can make adjustments to deal with having someone out of the office—and they do it willingly because they too might need the time, if not for a new child, perhaps to provide care to an older child, parent, or to take time for some personal medical need. "People rise to the occasion," said Eckblad. "It would be a myth to suggest that other people don't have to shoulder additional work or figure out how to reprioritize so that the things that are critical and time-sensitive occur. Yeah, that happens, and that's important to note, but it's worth it." AOC, and her staff, recognize and value that part of being human that includes a private life, family, and bringing new life into the world. The office policy makes that commitment real.[159]

And to support women, we also have to support men. Men too are parents and need to bond with their child—and should be expected to do so. So long as women are the only ones expected to nurture and care for children, they will be compensated less as employers assume that they will take time but men won't. AOC understands the well-documented fact that maternity leave adds to the pay gap between men and women, but parental leave helps alleviate it. For parents, the bonding process takes some time, learning how to take care of a new

---

159   Ibid.

life and adjust to this life-changing event. It should not be rushed—and if it is, that has negative consequences for both the parents and the child." As Eckblad noted, "There are these societal assumptions that are sometimes expressed and sometimes tacit that women are supposed to be the people who are in charge of childrearing and that's erroneous, that's based in patriarchy. We need to reimagine that frame and one way of doing so is saying: Men, women, mothers, fathers, are equally a part of this process."[160]

Men, women, mothers, and fathers are all part of the process. To move to a world in which that is actually our reality, women will have to take the lead. Women in support of women. Women helping other women. Women making sure that other women can shine. Our women's network must be vibrant. Often these networks are pitched just in terms of business and career opportunities, but what we are envisioning is much deeper than that—it's a philosophy and a lifestyle, embodied in shine theory. I shine a light on you, you shine one on her, she shines on me—we are all lit up! AOC's support of her friends when they are under attack, standing up for tipped workers, and making sure her staff get credit—and are fairly compensated—is her way of shining. That's the AOC way.

---

160 Ibid.

Conclusion

Putting things off is the biggest waste of life: it snatches away each day as it comes, and denies us the present by promising the future. The greatest obstacle to living is expectancy, which hangs upon tomorrow and loses today. You are arranging what lies in Fortune's control, and abandoning what lies in yours. What are you looking at? To what goal are you straining? The whole future lies in uncertainty: live immediately.

—Seneca, *On the Shortness of Life*[161]

IT MAY SEEM STRANGE TO quote a Roman philosopher in a book about a contemporary American politician at a time of great domestic turmoil, but the quote is apt. Life is finite, and we have only our time on this earth to make

---

161   Lucius Annaeus Seneca, *On The Shortness of Life*, Translated by Gareth D. Williams, accessed August 19, 2016, https://archive.org/stream/SenecaOnTheShortnessOfLife/Seneca+on+the+Shortness +of+Life_djvu.txt.

a difference. To maximize our short time, we learn lessons from others who have grabbed life by the horns and have worked to make the change that lies in their control. We learn from those who don't lose sleep worrying that they will be criticized for not waiting their turn, for defying stereotypes, for breaking the mold when necessary to have an impact. That's what AOC embodies, and that's why I have written this book.

AOC's life and how she lives it provide practical lessons as well as some inspiration considering how brief but impressive her career has been to date. AOC has demonstrated some key values and commitments on her way to success, such as believing in yourself and not letting haters take you off course, working hard and being prepared to prove your talents, bringing your experiences to your work by not forgetting how you got where you are, challenging the status quo, and staying true to your friends and allies. She's challenged assumptions about what young people, young women, young women and men of color, people from economically distressed backgrounds, immigrant families, and others are capable of— or how they should behave. She's not been willing to sit back and listen to the direction of her elders. Time is of the essence, she knows, for our nation and the world to deal with climate change, economic inequality, and corporate greed.

With an amazing swiftness, AOC has forged alliances and driven policy on some of the most consequential issues of our time, from the climate emergency and economic inequality to racism and misogyny, along the way challenging prejudices and conservative cultural mores about how young women, especially women of color, are supposed to behave. Her background, including a family that faced precarious economic circumstances because of her father's health issues and early death, has compelled her to fight for vulnerable populations, such as low-wage workers, immigrants, people of color, and younger people who face the dangers of rising temperatures and ocean waters as well as the political instability that will flow from that climate emergency. She may be a comic book hero, an influencer on social media, and a dynamic member of Congress, but AOC has lessons for all of us, especially women, who are fighting for an equal place in society and in our politics.

Leaning in is all very fine for women in the boardroom, but AOC recognizes that collective action is the necessary fuel for social change, not just self-improvement. What Ocasio-Cortez exemplifies is showing how women are stronger shoulder to shoulder, hand in hand, working for systemic fixes to wide-ranging problems but also standing up for each other as friends, colleagues, coworkers, and community members. She understands that the battle for justice and equality for women must include both nationwide changes that are necessary for women to thrive, especially women of color and women who face economic and other challenges, but also direct and immediate support for our friends, loved ones, and colleagues.

We are at a moral crossroads in our nation, with

many worried that the progress we have seen from the civil rights, women's rights, and LGBTQ+ rights battles is going to be undone. That's why we need to rally around each other and inspiring figures like Alexandria Ocasio-Cortez to retain hope and regain momentum. We cannot give up—AOC has stood up for justice and fairness, and we can't let her down. It's more than the specifics of the policies, the Green New Deal and Medicare for All or other ideas to transform our economy and our politics. What's really at stake is our vision of ourselves as actors, as doers, and as changemakers. AOC speaks to women and others who have not been in control of the power structure and says "you too can make a difference. You can be the ones who decide the future." Thus empowered, we can in fact ensure that our rights are not diminished and our future is not darkened.

Women like AOC will reshape America. They come from across the nation and are of all races, colors, and religions (including those who have no religion at all). We won't agree on everything—far from it! Women too can debate and disagree, but we will achieve major victories together. Each of us is necessary for the collective good.

Our fight for the future is one that must be joined by all people of goodwill who share that commitment to our core fundamental freedoms and protections, to the rights enshrined in our Constitution. It is important that we remind those who would sanctify the Founding Fathers that their work has been much improved upon and that many of the rights we hold dear came through outright war, legal and legislative campaigns, advocacy, civil dis-obedience, sit-ins, teach-ins, love-ins, speeches, marches, and most of all through the participation of Americans in the democratic process. Progress, by definition, is not static. And setbacks are frequent. That's why one of my favorite quotes is "eternal vigilance is the price of liber-ty."[162] Falsely attributed to Thomas Jefferson, it none-theless correctly captures how the work advocating for equality and justice is a never-ending project. And that's why so many have made that same point, even if in dif-ferent words. We can never rest and assume that our vic-tory is complete—protecting our rights and core values requires energy, commitment, but also the joy of engage-ment, indeed of battle. Dancing our own dance, living our fullest life, and protecting our friends and allies.

It used to be that women were subject to constant har-assment and groping and were expected to put up with it. In June 2019, E. Jean Carroll alleged that she had been raped by Donald Trump but had not had the strength at the time of the attack to come forward. That made her one of sixteen women to come forward with credible accusations of rape or sexual assault.[163] Two of the sixteen accused him of rape—in addition to E. Jean Carroll,

---

162 Thomas Jefferson Foundation, "Eternal Vigilance is the Price of Liberty (Spurious Quotation)," accessed August 16, 2019, https://www.monticello.org/site/research-and-collections/eternal-vigilance-price-liberty-spurious-quotation.
163 "The President Stands Accused of Rape Again," *The Economist*, June 29, 2019, https://www.economist.com/united-states/2019/06/29/the-president-stands-accused-of-rape-again.

Ivana Trump made rape an element of her divorce claims. Fearing to come forward, so many of these women recognized they had to speak out when Donald Trump was on his way to becoming president. Yet it did not stop him. Nevertheless, the fact that they have felt more at liberty to come forward does speak to positive changes in our culture. And younger women are much less willing to stay silent, which bodes well for us being able to shake free of a culture that has allowed women to be sexually abused and insulted without repercussions. Alexandria Ocasio-Cortez, the other newly elected women in Congress, and the women who have run for state office around the country—as well as many (but certainly not all) of their male colleagues of their generation—will not only refuse to put up with such behavior personally, but they are vouching for their friends, and, most importantly, recognizing that there is a public-policy and legal response that needs to be strengthened so there are real penalties for this type of discrimination and violence.

As Jessica Valenti commented on *Medium*, those white men who think that women and people of color gaining power and a voice is a direct threat to their own power find this moment very distressing. "Women—women of color, in particular—are amassing power across politics and culture, and those who have traditionally held that power are scared shitless," Valenti wrote. "Their hatred for Ocasio-Cortez, just like their pushback against #MeToo and the feminist movement, is a thin veil over what they really think, which is: *How dare they*. How dare women have the power to shape legislation? How dare they have the power to say no to sexual advances? How dare they hold men accountable? But they can't say those things, not out loud anyway—not without being taken to task. So instead, conservatives mock. And diminish. And discredit."[164]

President Trump has polished this mockery to a near art form to be imitated by his ditto-heads on Twitter, using insulting nicknames and describing women's bodies and faces in an unflattering way. All of which has done nothing to stop AOC and so many others from pushing back against misogyny and bullying. Twitter is a powerful tool, but we know how to wield it too. In fact, social media and viral videos, movies, music, and other real art forms are our strength, and we will not be outplayed by anyone trying to advance an agenda that glorifies gropers and racists.

There's a long to-do list for all of us, including making sure that the #MeToo moment becomes a movement and not something we remember with regret, thinking about "what could have been." No, instead it needs to represent a pivot point for transformational change when women, especially vulnerable women and women of color, collectively said "no more." No more bragging about sexual assault and groping, especially by elected officials and powerful men in media, business, and academia. No

---

164 Jessica Valenta, "Who's Afraid of AOC?" *Medium*, January 10, 2019, https://gen.medium.com/whos-afraid-of-aoc-ba3ac04d28b3.

more assuming that survivors of assault share in the blame and that men can still take office or stay in powerful jobs without suffering any consequences even when many women come forward with strong and substantiated accusations of harassment, assault, and even rape. No more will women be dismissed because they don't dress, or behave, or conform the way they are supposed to. And that no more will young women in positions of power get death threats on a daily basis, like what has happened to AOC and several of the other newly elected women of color in Congress. Fighting to make that a reality is the AOC Way.

The AOC Way embraces the idea that all people have a voice and a value, whatever our age, color, gender identity, religion, or other attribute—so long as we recognize the same humanity in others. "We the people"—those are the beautiful opening words of our Constitution. It's time to take them seriously.